About the book

Adam Morrell is a driver. A real, legally-licensed one. He's got a windscreen scraper and a little copy of the Highway Code and everything.

However for quite a while it looked like he might never pass his driving test. Nerves, bad preparation, strange instructors, some frankly baffling decision-making and even poor footwear selection all contributed to a litany of failures before he eventually succeeded in getting his licence.

Fortunately, it turned out he made all of those mistakes so that you don't have to. This book summarises all the tips and tricks Adam learned about learning to drive, so that you can go ahead and pass your driving test like a boss.

Sometimes, it's best to learn from the worst.

HOW TO PASS YOUR

DRIVING TEST LIKE A

BOSS

Adam Morrell

The way I see it, if you want the [driving licence], you gotta put up with

the [driving test].

-- Dolly Parton

Contents

Introduction

Hi, reader. Thanks for buying my book about driving. In the spirit of getting to know one another, I'd like to kick things off with a revelation about myself. Here is that revelation: I failed my driving test 5 (five) times.

In comparison, it only took five driving tests *in total* for crooning dreamboat squad One Direction - and I'm talking the full, original lineup here, complete with Zayn - to become a boyband completely and utterly licensed to drive, which meant that they were able to take turns behind the wheel while they were on tour. So yes, I'm technically a fraction of the person that Harry Styles and co are, which perhaps also explains why I'm still yet to successfully launch my own line of signature fragrances. One day.

Anyway, I passed my test on the sixth attempt, after five failures. *Well, that doesn't seem very boss-like*, you might be thinking.

And you would be correct. Those five fails aren't something I'm proud of. In fact, back when I was a single man I was so ashamed of my long-running failure to pass my test that I used to imply (and occasionally flat-out lie) to dates that I *could* drive, to prevent them from dumping me on the spot and jumping straight into the arms and passenger seat of the nearest qualified driver.

(A tip for anyone in a similar boat: I discovered that it's much easier to get away with being a secret non-driver if you live in London, because the wealth of frequent public transport options and lack of cheap and/or available parking mean that only fourteen people in the city find it practical to have a car (Harry Styles is one of them). Perhaps that's why so many people choose to move there; they're all secret non-drivers.

Thankfully but unsurprisingly, none of my dates ever called my bluff and asked me, mid-date, to back up my big-man driving talk by taking an impromptu solo trip on the motorway, reversing around a corner or renewing my car insurance. That would have put a dampener on what were intended to be romantic evenings, as well as foreshadowing a general compatibility problem that would have run far deeper than my inability to drive.

That said, I do remember taking my passport along to nightclubs and other events that might require me to present some form of ID, just so that I could save myself the indignity of having to present my little green provisional shame licence to a bouncer for inspection in front of my driving friends or work colleagues. In retrospect, it seems far, far stranger to take your passport with you to a foam party at a Stoke-on-Trent nightclub than to simply produce a provisional driving licence as ID.

Even until the last couple of years I found it quite difficult to talk to people I meet about my learning-to-drive experience. It was usually a guilty little secret that I kept hidden away alongside my love of *Don't Tell the Bride* (I'm a big fan of solid budget management) and the memory of my first day in a particularly corporate job where I misread the way my new managing director opened her office door to me, with an outstretched arm resting on the frame, as an invitation for a business hug and went in for the big embrace. It turned out it was not an invitation for a business hug.

The reason I'm so comfortable talking to you about it now (about learning to drive, anyway - the MD cuddle thing is still a bit too raw) and putting it all in writing is because over the last year I've made a conscious effort to talk to friends, family and colleagues about their own learning-to-drive experiences. And I quickly realised that I wasn't alone in finding those early days behind the wheel quite stressful. I've included some of those conversations about driving in the book, just to give you some extra perspective beyond that of the man who once became so flustered that he ran away in the middle of a driving lesson. See the next chapter for more on that.

If you're reading this, I'm going to assume you haven't passed your driving test yet, because this would be strange subject matter to be interested in otherwise. Perhaps you've taken your test previously and didn't pass, or maybe you're expecting to take your first one soon and getting a little nervous about it. Either way, I've been there, so you and I have something in common, as well as our shared passion for solid budget management.

So that's why I decided to write this book, aside from the groupies and the immense financial returns. The penny dropped while I was speaking to a friend of mine who also took a few times to pass their test. She told me she had recently realised that, back when she was learning to drive, it was really rare that she spoke to anyone who'd once been in as much turmoil about learning to drive as she was at that moment, but who'd passed their test and become a comfortable driver since. Everyone around her was either new to driving or so comfortable doing it that they'd forgotten what it was like to not know what you're doing. I reached for my typewriter.

So, I want to help you pass your driving test. I'm not going to teach you the technical elements of driving - I'm hoping you've found an instructor to help you with that part (more on that later). But in the rest of this book I humbly offer a few chapters of real-life advice and anecdotes gathered from my own rather mixed experiences, as well as some of my friends who I managed to corner over the last couple of months, to help give you the best chance of passing your driving test when the day arrives.

I know what you're thinking: *"Brilliant, the guy who failed five times is going to tell me how to pass my driving test."* And that's understandable. But it's also true that someone who has failed at something before they succeeded will be able to teach you more than someone who succeeded the first time. After all, wouldn't you rather invest your money in someone who finally created a successful start-up after a string of failures rather than a one hit wonder who may simply have gotten lucky first time?

The reality is that, if you channel them correctly, your struggles make you stronger. I made pretty much every mistake you can make before, during and after a driving test. Ultimately, in order to pass and to generally function behind the wheel thereafter, I had to articulate to myself what I was doing wrong and then figure out how to avoid making the same mistakes again. I really believe I'm a better driver now for having gone through that process. And the only thing better than learning from your own mistakes? Learning from somebody else's. Hence the book.

None of this means I don't still make the odd driving mistake now, by the way. I accidentally drove into my own wheelie bin a couple of weeks ago. Thankfully we both agreed it was an accident and took it no further. But in general, I'm a great driver; far better and far, far more at ease behind the wheel than I ever thought I would be back when I was 17 and struggling to understand why roundabouts made any sense to anyone. It gets easier.

Wherever you are in your driving education, I've been there - and from there, in the end, I passed my driving test. Eventually. At the sixth time of asking. But it doesn't matter how long it takes you to get there. It just matters that you do. Unless, of course, you're reading this book following the advent of driverless cars and the inevitable rise of the Autobots, but let's just assume you're not.

Also, a quick piece of housekeeping is to point out that I took my driving tests in the UK, so you may notice the odd difference if you're learning to drive elsewhere in the world. I can only apologise for my Britishness (which is just about the most British thing a person can do), but hopefully what I have to say is still relevant as the fundamentals of driving tend to be the same wherever you are.

Either way, if you remember just one thing from this book, let it be this: perseverance is the solution to almost every problem in life, whether you're trying to pass your driving test, learn to speak French, overcome writer's block, run a marathon, juggle knives, break into your dream career, put on a film night dedicated to a little-known character-actor or hug your company's managing director. If the thing you want is important enough to you and you keep plugging away, you'll get some kind of result eventually.

In short, whatever thing you want to do with your life, go out and do it. And if that thing right now is passing your driving test, let's get started.

Because if I can do it, *you* definitely can - as the next chapter should demonstrate in comprehensive fashion.

Lesson 1: How to Avoid Running Away from the Car

It does not matter how slowly you [learn to drive], so long as you do not

stop.

-- Confucius

I took my first driving lesson when I was 17 years old. In total the journey from that very first lesson to the day I finally passed my driving test took about 13 years. Except that it didn't really, because for a long time during that 13-year spell - immediately after ill-fated test number five, as it happens - I simply gave up on driving completely.

For years I struggled to figure out why it took so long for me to pass my driving test. Every single time my reason for failing seemed to be completely different. For example, the reason for my third test fail was that I had been driving too fast, whereas my fourth fail had been for driving too slowly. If only the DVLA had agreed to my very reasonable request for them to simply take an average from across the two tests, I might have built up a sweet decade of no-claims bonuses by now.

In all seriousness, I never had one of those unjust fails you occasionally hear about where someone claims their examiner penalised them for excessive blinking behind the wheel or something, all because they have a fail quota to fill at the diabolical behest of their cackling lizard-boss. No. My examiners were all fair, honest, usually bearded and only ever failed me completely justifiably. (Examiners are of course humans in general, so I'm sure mistakes on their part do occasionally happen, but the rate at which I hear those 'unfair fail' stories on driving test forums makes me suspect that many of those claiming this kind of thing happened to them are either lying to make themselves look better or have subconsciously repackaged the memory of the trauma to ease their damaged pride.) In case you're interested, I've included a more detailed rundown of my driving test fails as a humiliating appendix at the end of the book, so that's something to look forward to.

Strangely enough, the one thing I was sure of, even then - despite what you might see as evidence to the contrary - was that I wasn't failing because I was a bad driver. I was inexperienced of course, and that means that you do make the odd error, but in my driving lessons I would drive safely and more-or-less perfectly. The problem was that my ability and confidence in my lessons just didn't translate into my tests. After a while it started to feel like maybe I just wasn't meant to drive, so I didn't.

As with a lot of people, driving test nerves were the root of all my driving test problems. Anytime I had a test on the horizon, anxiety would get the better of me. It would start the night before the test, when I'd basically lie awake all night, gently panicking. With butterflies moshing in my stomach, I'd spend most of the night not sleeping until I was suitably drained of energy for my test whenever I woke up from whatever meagre slumber I'd been able to catch. And of course, that lack of sleep had its own effect, compounding my nerves and causing me to make poor decisions, react more slowly and make silly mistakes.

Another odd mental block I had when taking driving tests was that I just couldn't deal with the pressure of being observed doing something by a stranger. It's the same kind of phenomenon as when someone is sitting by you watching as you type something on a computer. You might be the Picasso of typing, tickling the keys with speed and accuracy when there are no eyes on you, but I guarantee that the second someone starts watching you, you'll make mistakes. Spell your own name incorrectly or continually get your own password wrong or something. Because as soon as someone is observing you, that's when even the simplest things become difficult. In psychology, this is known as the Hawthorne Effect; the idea that the act of observing something influences the outcome of that specific activity. In driving tests, it's known as a major inconvenience.

Anxiety is such an individual thing. It affects all of us, and it affects us all differently. I don't seem to suffer from those brain-scrambling nerves in any other area of my life except for driving. The only thing I can think of that's in any way comparable is when I worked for a very corporate company and had an authoritative sort of manager who intimidated me to the point that I once accidentally kicked her phone down the stairs. She was walking to a meeting with the phone balanced on her laptop, and it slid off as she went to open a door adjacent to a flight of stairs. Immediately behind her and permanently coiled for any opportunity to curry favour with her, I adopted a crane-like stance and tried to catch it with my foot. Sadly, I lacked opposable toes and happened to be wearing shoes that day, so I basically just booted her iPhone down to the next floor. At best it could have looked like a misjudged corporate powerplay, but I think I was basically just terrified of her while desperately wanting to impress her.

Anyway, for whatever reason, I had a specific nervousness about driving and driving tests. This was a surprise to me. I'm not what you would describe as a neurotic or nervous person. Usually I've always been calm and logical about things, whether I was delivering projects at work, public speaking or carrying a tray of drinks through a crowded foam party. But for some reason driving under supervision always got into my head in a way that dismantled my confidence. And when something lodges itself inside your head, it can be difficult to get it out of there.

Here's a story from the very recent past which I feel goes some way to summing up just how significant my driving test anxiety was.

Like I said, although I took my first driving lesson at 17, I only passed after I turned 30. This is because, after I failed my test for the fifth time, I took a long break from driving. That was partly due to circumstance - I followed my job to Birmingham and then to London, and the combination of having to pay more and more rent but also having access to better public transport meant it was easy for me to ignore the fact I couldn't legally drive. Life took over for a while, and I pretty much forgot about my green provisional licence in the meantime.

Some years I'd get fired up over Christmas and have a new year's resolution to give it another go, to finally start lessons again and get through my test. I knew that one day I'd be in a position where I needed to drive, whether for personal or professional reasons, and I intended to get ahead of that. But I just never did.

After my fifth failed test, probably 13 years passed before I sat in the driving seat again. I'm not exactly sure what the catalyst was for deciding to get my hands on the steering wheel again. I was living in Manchester by then and I'd turned 30 a couple of months earlier. I'd recently taken up running, which seemed to have become a kind of good-habit cornerstone in my life. Almost overnight, driving went from being the thing I kept at the back of my mind, next to memories of all the best Brendan Fraser quotes from *The Mummy*, to being pretty much the only thing I thought about.

When I eventually decided I wanted to give it another go, I knew I didn't want to go back to the one-lesson-a-week routine I'd tried and failed with the first time around. No, no, no. That system took too long to get me up to speed and gave me too much time to forget things. I wanted to absolutely immerse myself in driving for a short period of time so that I could break down my barriers and get through my next test.

So that's why I ended up opting for a three-day intensive course with a local instructor, a Ukrainian woman named Elena. The format of her course was straightforward; three consecutive 8-hour days of lessons followed by my driving test on the morning of the fourth day. The person who took my booking over the phone warned me that the schedule could be punishing, but I batted away his concerns. I could handle it. After all,

I'd failed my driving test five times and had last sat behind the wheel of a car more than a decade previously. How hard could it be?

It turned out the answer to that question was *Quite hard indeed.*

I'll set the scene. It was day one of my intensive course and Elena and I were perhaps three hours into the session. With the seconds palpably elapsing before my test in three days' time, Elena was pushing me hard with - I believe it is fair to say - her very 'robust' communication style. She was jabbing her finger at me, throwing her hands in the air and slapping her forehead with frustration at seemingly everything I did. After three hours of that on the back of not having driven at all for 13 years, I was frazzled and finding it difficult to consistently perform even the most basic of manoeuvres.

This all escalated to the point that I tried to turn right at some traffic lights and messed it up. I think I cut across the junction or something. Elena's constant pecking and tutting was necessary because of the extremely tight deadline I'd set myself, but by this point in my descent into a driving delirium her prodding just seemed relentless and unfair. Something inside me stopped ticking. I flicked on the indicator, pulled over and turned off the engine.

"I'm sorry, Elena - I can't do this anymore," I said, like a romcom leading man who's just realised his arrogant fiancé isn't right for him and his ideal woman had been his kind-hearted, bespectacled office assistant all along. Then I exited the car and started sprinting away, leaving a bemused Elena sitting in the passenger seat of her now-driverless car. (And yes, having checked the dates, this does mean I technically own the rights to driverless cars everywhere.)

To summarise, I was so stressed by a driving lesson that I literally got out of my instructor's car and ran away. Like a boss. Let me remind you: at the time in my life when this happened, I was a thirty year-old man with my own flat, holding down a responsible job where I managed a number of people, and generally proving pretty successful at surviving. But in that particular moment, when it came to making a car turn right, I had an uncontrollable urge to run away and hide.

Smart as a whip, I deliberately ran away uphill in the opposite direction to where the car was pointing. I figured that the U-turn required would earn me crucial seconds if Elena tried to come after me. There were two downsides to this strategy:

1. I'd chosen to abandon the car on a random industrial estate on the outskirts of Manchester. There seemed to be nothing but a post-apocalyptic sea of abandoned warehouses around me. The scene was like something out of Mad Max and I had absolutely no idea where I was.

2.   It's a lot more tiring to run uphill than downhill.

I carried on running. I rounded a corner. Then down an alley which brought me out on a different road. And then I saw Elena driving towards me. "Adam!" she called, her head sticking out of the window like she was an excited puppy. Still in a blind panic, I spun around and sprinted back up the same alley in the direction I'd just come from as she drove past to the top of the road.

I was literally running around in circles. By the time I'd dashed to the end of the alley, Elena and her car were already there waiting, and trundled along gently next to me as my run slowed to a pathetic jog. It was one of the worst car chases of all time; me sweating and gasping at the sky as Elena drove slowly next to me shouting encouraging things like, "Adam, come back. It's OK. Get back in the car". It seemed impossible to escape her on foot. I guess the difficulty I was experiencing outlines one of the key benefits of driving a car over trying to run everywhere like a deranged Mo Farah; it's much easier on the lungs.

A group of workmen had appeared further down the road and were now watching the pair of us, a sweaty, thirty-something man on foot being slowly pursued down the road by an elderly Ukrainian lady gently calling to him from the window of her Ford Focus learner car.

To cut a long story short, I got back in the car, where Elena pulled over and talked to me for a while about how she became an instructor. About how, growing up, she used to be a performer in the circus in the Ukraine, where her family and friends and even her own brain told her she'd never be able to achieve her childhood dream of becoming a driving instructor, and yet here she was, behind the wheel of her own learner car, pursuing a pupil sprinting anxiously around an industrial estate. She may have embellished the story for inspirational effect, but it did get through to me. I needed to stop listening to the doubting voice in my head.

After Elena dropped me home that evening, I spent some time researching how to manage nerves. Nothing like that had never happened to me before. In almost every part of my life I'm wired for logic and efficiency (to the point that, recently, while using the electric hand dryer in the work bathrooms, I instinctively started to turn around mid-dry so that I would finish the process with my hands pointing back behind me, and then be facing the right way to walk straight out of the door when the dryer finishes. I only realised when someone walked in as I was in this position that it probably looked as though I was drying my bum, so I've stopped doing it now). But in that moment I'd basically suffered a panic attack, and I didn't want that to happen again.

So, for each of the ensuing days, before Elena picked me up for my full-day lessons and ultimately my test, I tried a few different things to help settle my nerves for the day of driving ahead. I've shared my process here but no two people are the same, so I would encourage you to try different methods to find what helps you the most.

1. Breathe. Count down slowly from 10 to 0. With each number, take one complete breath, inhaling and exhaling. For example, breathe in deeply, saying "10" to yourself. Breathe out slowly. On your next breath, say "nine", and so on. If you feel light-headed, count down more slowly to space your breaths further apart. When you reach zero, you should feel more relaxed. If not, try different breathing exercises until you find one that works for you. Breathing is important. Get good at it.

2. Find a dog and play with it. This is a little more leftfield as an anxiety management measure and probably not practical in every situation, but it worked for me. Dogs are wonderful and don't worry about things like driving tests or oral hygiene or the future; they just want to live in the moment with you. If you're looking for more specific guidance, I used a local sausage dog but I presume any household pet works just as well.

3. Get outside and go for a walk. Fresh air works wonders for clearing your head and putting one foot in front of the other helps to organise your thoughts. Also, you'll build up your hind legs for working the car pedals.

4. Write things down. There's something powerful about putting your thoughts on paper and reading them back. I've told dozens of people that same story about me running away from a driving lesson for years, but it's only while writing this book and making light of it on a page that I've realised I actually had a panic attack that day, and I'm fine with it. Plus - if nothing else - you'll have the basis of a wildly successful eBook on your hands afterwards.

5. Remember, it's all fine. Driving licences aren't a finite, dwindling resource that we're running out of. Even if this next driving test doesn't work out, you'll get there eventually. You want to pass the test this time, sure - but if you don't, you'll pass a test in the future provided you just keep trying. The only thing that can truly stop you is you.

Ultimately, nerves are a great thing because they're a sign that what you're doing matters to you. And that's exactly what you should be doing with your life. You don't want to be rid of your nerves entirely, because that would mean you don't truly care about what you're doing.

The problem with putting your heart into something means that it's easy to take setbacks from that thing to heart. So, it's important that when we're feeling anxious about something important to us and that fight or flight moment arrives, we can handle it.

Everyone's wired differently and it's impossible to tell how we'll react to anything until we personally are in that situation. If you'd have asked me back when I was a typical know-it-all 16-year-old, I'd have staked every football sticker I owned that I'd never have a driving lesson experience so stressful that it would literally repel me away from the car, but on that fateful day my overpowering instinct was to run in the opposite direction and I couldn't do anything about it.

When the dust settled however - after Elena had run me to ground and forced me back into the car - I was able to centre myself and come back swinging. That's what it's all about; getting back on the horse/car.

It can take practice to improve how you handle your nerves and I wouldn't necessarily recommend trying to learn those skills on the fly during a 3-day intensive driving course. But I do recommend pushing yourself out of your comfort zone as part of your routine to build up your tolerance.

Make it your goal to put yourself in positions that scare you and you'll find you get used to mastering the fear when the adrenaline starts pumping through your veins. You'll bolster your overall resilience as a result. There's a lot of ways to do this, I think. Give a presentation to a group of people, take singing lessons, do a skydive, go on a rollercoaster, start your own podcast or YouTube channel, enter a 10k run, do an open mic comedy night, shave your head, hold a snake, go to a Zumba class, write some poetry and show it to someone, audition for Britain's Got Talent. Surprise yourself. Do something you wouldn't expect yourself to do.

If you're in a controlled environment, nothing can go wrong (apart from the skydive I guess - be careful with that one). Worst-case scenario, you might get a bit embarrassed in front of some people you may never meet again, and you'll end up with a self-deprecating anecdote to entertain your friends. Best-case scenario, you make yourself a stronger person and find a new hobby, such as snake-holding.

It's sometimes difficult to replicate the conditions of a real driving test if you're very comfortable with your instructor. A friend of mine found it useful to have a mock test the night before her actual one, which she would book with a different driving instructor – someone she wasn't already familiar and friendly with, and who used a different car. There's something about switching things up that's good for making you concentrate and practice getting comfortable with being uncomfortable. Going back to the car she'd been driving continually for three days the following morning helped her to relax a lot.

In some ways, this might seem an oddly pessimistic opening chapter to a book designed to help you pass your driving test. It might seem downbeat to start off by talking about managing anxiety and coping with failure, but I think it's important to internalise that the worst-case scenario of taking your driving test is that you fail your driving test. The world doesn't end if you wake up the next day with a green licence. And it's only a failure if you give up.

*

TL; DR

DO acknowledge your nerves. You're feeling them because you care about the thing you're doing, and you want to do it well. Try to keep things in perspective and channel that nervous energy into making the most of your driving education. The whole point of learning is that you will get things wrong occasionally, so don't worry about not being perfect.

DON'T run away from the car, figuratively or literally. You're learning something new. Sometimes it'll be hard, but nothing worthwhile ever came quickly or easily. Sure, take a break from learning to drive if you need to; just don't give up on it. You'll get there.

Conversations About Driving: Jona

Jona is one of my closest friends. We met through work about 10 years ago and he was one of the best men at my wedding. And yes, the story about me running away from a driving lesson made an appearance during his speech.

A quick non-driving story to introduce him. Jona and I are both film fans, to the extent that we once stood outside the main party tent at a music festival talking to each other 1:1 about *Mrs Doubtfire* for upwards of an hour and a half - only a slightly shorter duration than the film itself. Anyway, a few years ago he and I attended a sci-fi movie all-nighter at the Prince Charles Cinema in London. The event started at 7pm on Saturday night and ended at around 8am the next morning.

It was really good: the first movie we saw was Danny Boyle's *Sunshine*, a great movie with a great Benedict Wong performance. Then we saw Benedict Wong's name come up again in the opening credits for *Moon*. Pretty much in unison, we said something along the lines of: "Well, hang on, is this a sci-fi all-nighter or a Benedict Wong all-nighter?". We checked at the desk and it was indeed a sci-fi all-nighter, as advertised.

But after the event we looked up Benedict Wong on Wikipedia and saw that he'd been in loads of other great movies, plus *Prometheus*. And so we decided that we should put on a Benedict Wong all-nighter, and it should be called 'All Night Wong' and we'd serve Wong Island Iced Teas at the bar. Maybe we could have a 'Wong-Along', where we'd do some bespoke subtitling so that everyone could join in with Benedict Wong's lines as he spoke then on screen.

Ultimately it turned out that we were still quite drunk and tired when we came up with the idea, and it also transpired that screening films is quite expensive, so it didn't happen in the end. But it's nice that I was able to bring both Jona and Benedict Wong into this project at least.

Anyway, on with the driving chat, which took place during a slightly hungover walk around Clapham Common one morning while I was visiting Jona in London.

*

Adam: Hello, Jona. When did you learn to drive?

Jona: Hello, Adam. I started taking lessons when I was 17. My brother, who's a year older than me, was really keen to learn and get a car, and he saved up to buy this Ford Fiesta that he was going to drive as soon as he passed. He just really wanted to get behind the wheel. But I wasn't really that fussed because, well, I wasn't all that fussed about anything when I was 17. But basically what happened was that my mum told me that it was important and kind of forced me into it. I'm glad she did though.

Adam: Yeah, I wasn't the keenest to get behind the wheel either. Who was your instructor?

Jona: I used the same guy that my brother learned with. He was fine, a bit eccentric. During one lesson I mentioned to him that I was learning guitar and he immediately pulled out a harmonica from the glove compartment and started playing it, so that was good. My mum also took me out a bit on an industrial estate to practice manoeuvres and stuff, and then out on the roads when I got a bit more confident. That was useful, to get that extra practice outside of lessons. She didn't use a harmonica though.

Adam: How did you take to driving then?

Jona: Not very well. I can't really remember my lessons at all, but I know that I passed third time. The first test I just wasn't ready for. I think I failed that one for speeding. On my second test, literally the first thing the examiner asked me to do was to reverse into a parking space. I'm not sure I'd even done that manoeuvre before, and I was really nervous and completely messed it up, essentially, so I failed that test immediately then had to do the rest of it knowing I wasn't going to pass.

Adam: What do you remember about taking the test you passed?

Jona: Well, I remember my friend Paul and I had tickets to see Harry Hill in Windsor that evening…

Adam: Obviously.

Jona: Yeah, and we didn't really have a plan to get there if I didn't pass my test. Fortunately I did, but then I was a bit overconfident and went straight on the motorway. I also accidentally clipped a load of wing mirrors on this little road in Windsor. Sorry to anyone reading this who was a victim of that. I don't think there was any damage done.

Adam: Did anyone give you any good advice while you were learning to drive?

Jona: My dad gave me some good parallel parking advice, actually. He basically told me to imagine the car from above while I was moving it around, a bit like old school Grand Theft Auto, because that makes it a bit easier. He was right, so now I do that when I'm parking, or when I'm playing modern Grand Theft Auto.

I also went on a speed awareness course a little while ago and a couple of things stayed with me from that.

Adam: OK, like what?

Jona: One thing they drilled into us was that all the speed cameras, electric speed detection boards, extra signage and so on, that all costs money. And councils don't have a lot of money to throw around, so when they spend it, they really need to justify it. So, when you see a lot of speed prevention measures somewhere, it's more than likely that people have died there. That's a sobering thought.

The other thing that stuck with me is that a really high proportion of car accidents happen within a couple of miles of where the driver lives. You know, they're nearly home, they're in a familiar area and they get complacent. So, it's important to stay switched on. It's changed how I drive for sure.

Adam: That's good advice. What would you say to someone who was a little worried about taking their driving test?

Jona: I'd say that a load of people can drive, so it can't be that hard, can it?

Adam: Very true. So, I want this book to be kind of light-hearted as well as useful. Do you have any stories about driving since you passed your test?

Jona: Well, I had a bit of misfortune with my first car, which was actually the Fiesta my brother had saved up to buy back when he was learning to drive. I think he'd just bought a new car so my mum decided that he should give the Fiesta to me, even though my brother was the one who'd saved up and bought it. He was delighted about that as you might imagine.

Adam: Your brother does respond well to authority. [Note: He does not.]

Jona: Incorrect. So, I'd been driving the Fiesta for a couple of months, but then one morning it wouldn't start. We were pushing it up the road to get it going, but nothing was happening. I looked under the bonnet and discovered someone had stolen the battery.

Adam: Amazing.

Jona: Then another time, once we'd had a battery put back in there, I took it to the garage for some reason. I was complaining about my spark plugs or whatever and the mechanic suddenly said: "You do realise you've got no number plates on?" They'd been stolen.

Adam: This must have been a Fiesta worth having.

Jona: It really wasn't. And then one other time I was out and about, driving the car. And I think maybe a week before I'd had the AA out for something, and they'd told me not to drive the car, because something needed to be fixed. But anyway, I needed to get somewhere so I just took the chance, and the car broke down. So, I rang the AA, and they wouldn't come out because they'd told me not to drive it, so I had to walk an hour and a half to Maidenhead to get to wherever I was going. Eventually I got back to get the car and somehow it had been stolen.

Adam: That's incredible. It'd be great if all of the theft was by the same person in a really gradual heist. Maybe they put the first battery back in so they could drive it away.

Jona: I can only assume it was the same people who'd taken the battery and number plates, yes, gradually stealing the car piece by piece and reassembling it somewhere. They must have got bored or cocky and just come back for the rest of it in one go.

Adam: At least they'll never be able to take the memories. Thank you very much for your time, Jona.

Lesson 2: How to Find Your Mentor

If the [alternative driving instructor] is more fly, then you must buy.

-- Snoop Dogg

One other thing I learned during that proud day on which I bailed out of and ran away from my driving instructor's car (aside from the fact I had a pressing need to increase my lung capacity) was the value of a great teacher. To this day I have no idea if Elena actually *believed* I would or could pass my imminent driving test as she was coaxing me back into the car to carry on. I suspect at that point she wasn't even sure I'd make it back to my house without having a complete breakdown. But she made *me* believe I could do it. So, I did.

Don't waste your time with an instructor who makes you doubt yourself. I did exactly this in my early driving career and I can't tell you how much it held me back.

I kept the same instructor - let's call him Pete, because that was his name - for each of my first five failed driving tests. In hindsight that sounds like a bad call on my part at best. For starters, it's Einstein's definition of insanity - doing exactly the same thing over and over again, expecting a different result. And no one sets out thinking that insanity is a good strategy for passing their driving test.

However, at the time I felt a level of obligation to see my learning-to-drive journey through with Pete. He was local. I occasionally saw him around town; he'd even gotten to know my parents a little bit. He'd almost become a member of the family. Not a close member or one that anyone particularly liked, but family all the same.

He was probably more like a partner you'd been drifting away from for a while and who you really wanted to break up with, but who was still really quite into you. Pete was my first, my driving day-one from my driving day-one, and because of that I had difficulty ending things with.

I still remember that first driving lesson vividly. Pete, my shiny new instructor, still in all his original packaging, had arranged to pick me up at home after I'd returned from college in the afternoon. It was a sunny spring day and I wore my Port Vale slippers as I watched out of the window for him. I hardly ever wore slippers, but my parents had told me that my thick trainer soles would made it hard to feel the car pedals, and so I'd followed their guidance and decided to drive in my slippers, like a lunatic.

Eventually, Pete pulled up outside the house in his black Ford Fiesta and strode over to our door, smartly dressed in a grey suit and a red shirt.

I would come to learn that Pete wore this exact same outfit for every first lesson with a new pupil, oddly similar to the way that Tiger Woods always wears a red shirt with black trousers for the final round of each major golf tournament he plays in. But there are no notable driving stories about Tiger Woods, so I'll move on.

For the rest of the time I knew him, Pete dressed as though he'd spent the morning rolling around in Millets, and would routinely turn up covered in combat trousers, windbreakers, beanies and hiking boots. I didn't know that at the time though so I hadn't realised he would be smartly dressed for my first lesson. Thinking this must be going to be a more formal event than I'd anticipated, I quickly threw on a hoodie that was normally reserved "for best" and ran down the stairs to answer the door. I passed my mum on the landing. She immediately clocked the sacred hoodie. "It's not a fashion show, Adam", she called after me, perhaps rolling her eyes at her diva son's flamboyant decision to wear his finest hooded jumper to his first driving lesson. Just to reiterate, I was wearing a hoodie, jogging trousers and Port Vale slippers. The catwalk king. I kissed her goodbye and stepped out to meet Pete.

What followed was, I think, a fairly typical first driving lesson. Pete drove us to a quiet little spot next to some fields near my house, where he parked up and invited me to step out of the car and walk with him. I felt like a Jane Austen character. The picturesque setting suggested he was either going to try to inspire me or propose to me. It turned out he just wanted us to walk 20 metres away from the car and then turn around so he could check I could read the number plate from a distance.

After I passed the eyesight test he led me back to the car and ushered me into the driving seat, and then we spent the rest of the lesson driving very slowly around Stoke-on-Trent, both dressed to kill; he in his Burton suit and I in my hoodie from Hanley market. I didn't exactly take to my first time driving like a duck to water, but aside from a couple of hairy moments at the Smallthorne roundabout medley I did OK.

Pete's driving seat had some kind of beaded cover over it. I'm not sure whether it was a lumber aid or if he just really liked the bohemian look of the thing. Either way, when I got home, I realised I'd been sweating against it to the point that the back of my hoodie now looked like it had been printed in a fetching leopard skin pattern. I can confirm my mum was not happy about having to wash my best hoody after just one outing.

*

Like many great footballers who go on to become mediocre coaches, Pete proved to be a perfect example of someone who was himself good at the thing he taught, but just wasn't a natural teacher of it to other people. He was a fine driver, which is the absolute minimum I expect from a driving instructor, but he was also short-tempered and would frequently get frustrated if I made a mistake, as though it was a personal insult to him. More than once he had to ask me to park up while he took a walk to 'clear his head'.

He did have things going on in his personal life which perhaps served to make him so rash and unpredictable in his tutoring. They also seemed to make him hungry. Frequently he'd direct me to a local chip shop during a lesson and have me park up outside for ten minutes while he ambled in to pick up a lunchtime special for himself. (He never offered to get me anything - our relationship was purely professional.) As a 17-year-old boy, never having had any other driving tuition and also being something of a moron, I assumed this was how everyone learned to drive; receiving rewards for good manoeuvres with the odd chip or chunk of battered sausage from their instructor's lunchtime special, a bit like how one might train an increasingly chubby puppy.

To his credit, Pete did bring to the table some superb turns of phrase, generally to do with the level of exertion he wanted me to apply to the steering wheel. These included "Yeah, go on! Pull the wheel - pull it like you're pulling a man off your lady" (implication: turn the wheel with some urgency), and "Alright, now just nudge it the width of a gnat's knacker" (turn the wheel a small amount).

Sadly for me though, Pete was generally more about the stick than the carrot, or the battered sausage. I remember the morning of my third test, on which he had me practicing my manoeuvres one last time before we headed to the test centre. I accidentally hit the curb while reversing around a corner - something I never normally messed up - and he absolutely tore me to shreds, literally shouting at me from the passenger seat.

I don't know if he believed the dressing-down would motivate me, but in hindsight I would say he should have deduced from the fact that I was learning to drive in my slippers that I probably wasn't the type of pupil who would respond well to tough love. We arrived at the test centre half an hour later, checked in and sat down quietly in the waiting room with two or three other learners and their instructors, with my bottom lip still quivering a bit. I remember 'Sexed Up' by Robbie Williams was playing on the radio and that the other people's instructors didn't look as though they'd been screaming at their pupils half an hour earlier. I already knew I wasn't going to pass that test. It does however seem somewhat fitting that I, now an openly bald man, saw no benefit whatsoever from the hairdryer treatment.

I guess what I'm saying is that teaching isn't for everyone, and not every teacher is right for you. It's not a sign of weakness to tell an instructor you don't feel they're the best fit for you, or that you've decided to try a different approach. It might sometimes be difficult to do that, but it makes life easier in the long run. Think of it from your instructor's perspective too: they don't want to spend time teaching someone that they struggle to help.

You may already have a driving instructor you're very happy with. In that case, feel free to skip ahead to the next chapter, which is all about maximising what you learn in your lessons. However, if you've not yet found the right teacher or you're on the fence about switching, here's my tips on what to look for:

1.   The price. It's an unavoidable factor but the truth is that learning to drive with a professional is relatively expensive whoever you go with. For me, saving £2 per lesson by going with the cheapest

instructor I could find was a false economy. In total I probably had around 60 driving lessons with Pete, which by using my calculator I can tell you equates to around £1200 over two and a half years. Most of my friends passed after 30 or 40 hours. At that volume I could have paid 50% more per lesson and my overall outlay would have been 33% less. It's not an exact science, but my advice would be not to pick or stay with an instructor just because they're the cheapest per hour - it may well be that they're not actually the most cost-effective choice.

2. The car. Most instructors will have one car for you to learn in, unless they're showing off. As a learner it can be hard to vet your instructor's car without physically sitting in it. This is why it's best to have a trial lesson with someone before committing to any kind of block booking. If you're in a position to be able to practice in another car outside of your instructor lessons, you ideally want to be able to learn in a car reasonably similar to the one you'll do your other practice in, just for consistency. When you do take lessons in a different car, look out for how your instructor coaches you using markers inside the car. Pete was very good at pointing out how reversing around a corner could be done by tracking the edge of the curb against a particular part

of the back-windscreen wiper. When parallel parking, Elena would ask me to stop the car and look at where the corner of where the other vehicle sat in my rear window. Eventually you'll intuitively be able to put the car where you want it, but until then the markers are a big help.

3. The person. Personality and chemistry between the two of you is key. You're going to spend quite a few hours trapped together in a car, so try to pick someone you can talk to and who you're going to be able to take criticism from. It's an important part of learning. And try to make sure they care about what they're doing. If you don't get the feeling your instructor is at least partly motivated by helping you to pass your test, what chance do you have?

4. The approach. Let me just say that if you're considering an intensive course with very little recent driving behind you, you might want to ease yourself in with a few refresher lessons as an on-ramp, or you too could find yourself fleeing across an industrial estate with your bewildered instructor pootling along behind you.

Above everything else, trust your instincts; sometimes, you just get a feeling. Once, when I was living in London, I noticed an intensive driving school by the name of Crash Course Driving, bizarrely with the 'Crash' part stylised like a Batman cartoon 'Pow'-type impact graphic. I'm afraid that just didn't fill me with confidence that they could supply the mentorship I needed.

And if by some chance your internal jury is still out on the instructor you're learning with, it can be good to get a second opinion on how they're doing with you. Don't worry, you don't need to plant hidden cameras in the car. Just book a session or two with a different instructor and see if they point out any crucial gaps in your understanding or skill set that you should have down by now. Or just plant hidden cameras in the car, whatever works.

Ultimately, if your instructor's style isn't working out for you or they don't make you believe in yourself for whatever reason, you need to end the relationship and go with someone else. You're both grown-ups, one of whom is paying the other for their time; time which could be better spent elsewhere. Don't persevere and blindly hope that things work out. Life's too short to spend it with people who don't bring out the best in you.

*

TL; DR

DO put your foot down if your instructor isn't right for you. Grasp the nettle and have the conversation. It can be hard, but it will be better for you in the long run. And definitely don't buy a big block of driving lessons with anyone you've not already spent a couple of trial lessons with.

DON'T pick or stay with an instructor purely because they're the cheapest option per hour. If you don't learn well with that person, you'll take longer to get up to test standard and you might end up taking more tests than you would have done had you chosen a more suitable instructor. As much as possible, try to focus on finding the right person.

Conversations About Driving: JK

JK is a man I used to work with. Don't judge him for being called JK. It wasn't a choice on his part; it was a nickname our office gave him to distinguish him from the several other Jameses we already employed, largely a result of the baby-James uprising of the late 80s. It wasn't his fault.

JK originally joined the company on a graduate scheme and on the day he was introduced to me I went to shake his hand, only to discover he'd forgotten he was already holding a pen in there and nearly stabbed me through the palm with it. He assured me it was an accident rather than a corporate powerplay, though I made a mental note to kick his phone in the stairs in retaliation if he stepped out of line again.

We were both fortunate enough and immature enough to have a pool table at the digital marketing agency we worked for, and this was to become the setting for a weird ritual JK and I would carry out each time we played each other, in order to decide who would break. I'm not quite sure where it came from - possibly the absence of an actual coin - but he and I invented an honesty-based imaginary coin toss system. Basically, one of us would think of one side of a coin and the other had to guess what it was. When you think about it, the fact that a real coin is needed to evidence the result of the toss highlights the duplicity and dishonesty that is rife in our society.

JK is about ten years younger than me, physically at least, so I was interested in his generational perspective on learning to drive. Sadly, he and I no longer work together, but I was able to corner him one lunchtime during his final week to have a conversation about driving. Don't worry, he sorts out his lunch during the chat.

*

Adam: So JK, how long have you been driving?

JK: Since I was 17, so six or seven years now.

Adam: OK, so you started learning at 17.

JK: Yeah, I was at sixth form, doing my AS levels.

Adam: How did you take to driving?

JK: I was the youngest in my year, so I was in a rush to get on with it. I'd spent the whole year being driven around by my friends who'd passed.

Adam: I had about thirteen years of that.

JK: So, when I turned 17 I had my theory test booked two weeks later and had driving lessons lined up, so I was pretty quick on it. I think I took double driving lessons, so instead of doing just the one hour I'd do two hours at once, so I'd spend less time driving back and forth from my house.

Adam: Right, so you were able to get out further and drive in different places before you headed back? That's a good tip.

JK: Yeah, I wanted to squeeze as much out of it as I could, and it was good for getting me a bit more comfortable driving in unfamiliar places I think.

Adam: Makes sense. Who taught you to drive?

JK: My driving instructor was a guy called Mark. He was an ex-fireman... Well, he was a fireman at the time actually, but he was teaching people to drive part-time alongside that.

Adam: How did you happen across him then?

JK: He was a recommendation from a friend of mine. His dad was friends with the instructor, so he taught my friend to drive and then he told me about him. He did warn me though that the instructor was an absolute lad. A real bloke, you know, and probably not in the best way.

Adam: Oh really?

JK: Well, I remember once we were just driving around and - I don't know how explicit I can be?

Adam: Please, be as explicit as you like.

JK: OK, we were coming up to this roundabout and waiting for the traffic to go, so he was all like, keep left, you've got to give way to the right and all that. And then this woman drove past us and he pointed at her and was like "I [romanced] her".

Adam: That *is* quite explicit. I might change that to 'romanced' for the book.

JK: That's fair enough. So, I was just like, "Great, OK then", and we carried on. Just awful stuff like that. He had no problems talking about his sex life.

Adam: Maybe he was just trying to put you at ease.

JK: He did this thing for me; you know how you need to be really clearly checking your wing mirrors all the time in your test? Well, I wasn't doing it, so he cut out some Page 3 models and stuck them next to the wing mirrors of the car.

Adam: Good lord.

JK: I told you, he was an absolute pervert. But to be fair he was marketed to me as a lad's lad which I suppose he turned out to be.

Adam: Came as described.

JK: Yes, came as described, complete with boobs on his mirrors. He had me driving like that for a good few weeks. "You might want to check out that mirror over there again".

Adam: I can't say I've heard that one before, but it's an interesting tip. Can you remember your first driving lesson? Anything stick out from it?

JK: Yeah, he brought a dinner plate with him, so I could practice feeding the steering wheel through my hands.

Adam: Haha!

JK: We went round the corner from where I lived, and there's this long straight road that he had me practicing changing gears and finding the bite on the clutch and stuff. And at the end of the road there's a big car park that was empty at the time, so he had me turning in there and practicing feeding the wheel. And I was doing a terrible job of it, basically, so he told me to get out, get in the passenger seat next to him instead and practice with this dinner plate he'd brought.

Adam: Superb. So, you were just there, manhandling a dinner plate while you were parked up?

JK: Yep. On my first driving lesson, we parked up two miles from my house, and I practiced gripping a dinner plate. It did work though in the end to be fair. After he dropped me home, he told me to carry on practicing with one of my own dinner plates so I just sat at home doing that before my next lesson, and then I was fine after that.

Adam: Did you pass your test first time?

JK: I didn't. I passed second time. My first test was annoying, because I failed during the preamble to a reverse around a corner. When I was pulling up, some moody guy was pulling out of the road I was going to reverse into, and because I'd indicated too soon, before the actual turning, he went to pull out and I'd caused a hazard. I should have indicated after I'd passed the corner, but because I'd done it before he'd assumed I was turning in there and that he could go.

Adam: It's so annoying, isn't it? Failing really early on and still having to finish the test?

JK: Yeah, because I did know it. It was like, can't I go home and give up? I'm just wasting my time here.

Adam: Sure.

JK: Plus, the examiner who I got for my test was Barry the Bastard.

Adam: His real name, I assume?

JK: He was a local guy at the test centre, and everyone knew that if you get Barry for your first time, you're getting failed. And sure enough I did - which was my own fault obviously, but people always had stories about how it was Barry and his bastardry that meant they failed.

Adam: So, you took your second test pretty soon after that?

JK: Yeah, I took it as soon as I could, basically went home and booked it straight away because I was ready and confident and all that. And that one went fine, just a couple of minors at roundabouts, things like that.

Adam: So, what did you do after you'd passed?

JK: I sat about in the test centre until my mum brought my little Polo that we'd bought to pick me up and got me insured, and I drove home from the test centre in that.

And then I got home. There's a funny little tradition in our family - I've no idea where it came from - but it's a letter that my mum gave to us, basically talking about the honour and the privilege of driving, and the freedom it brings. It's a nice little thing, all my brothers had gotten it before me when they passed. It also had some pieces of advice in it, things that they don't tell you when you're learning to drive, and I remember one thing was when you're driving past someone walking with a child, take your foot off the gas and just rest it on the brakes, because you never know, they might suddenly run out into the road. Little stories and anecdotes like that. Just a couple of little pages that my brothers and sister and I have all got. It's a sweet little thing. Very wholesome.

Adam: That's really nice.

[At this point our colleague Sian comes into the room, looking for JK]

Sian: Sorry JK, I've got Rach [another colleague of ours] on the phone for you. Do you know what it'll be about?

JK: [Slightly embarrassed laugh] Yeah, it'll be about my, erm, my lunch. Erm.

[JK pauses, clearly caught between not wanting to break off our interview but also not wanting to jeopardise his lunch.]

Adam: Go for it.

JK: I'll just jump out for a second. It's just about whether she's going to get me mac and cheese or not from M&S. I'll be back in a second.

[JK leaves. I'm left on my own in the meeting room, contemplating Barry the Bastard and Mark, the maverick fireman-turned-driving-instructor whose methods include wing mirror pornography. It's a nice moment.]

JK: Hi, I'm back. Went for the beef ragu in the end.

Adam: Good choice. OK, so did you get any useful advice when you were learning to drive?

JK: Aside from what was in that letter, my driving instructor told me I'd never again drive like I did in my driving test, which was true. He was a...

Adam: A pervert?

JK: A pervert, yes, but also a fireman. And I never took my Pass Plus with him, but what I did do was go out with him after I passed, and he showed me how you speed safely, because that's what he'd do when driving a fire engine on emergency response and all that.

Adam: That sounds interesting.

JK: Yeah, he didn't actually have me driving over the speed limit or anything, but he sat in the car beside me and went through his thought process as we went along. I just remember him looking ahead and he'd be going, "Car pulling out over there, woman waiting at the traffic lights which might go red, bike coming around that corner so someone might be overtaking that in a second", talking so fast, almost like a rapper or an auctioneer. But his point was that if you're driving recklessly, or at the speed you'd be driving a fire truck, that's the speed you'd have to think at to do it safely. I think his point was "You can't think like this, because you've not had this experience," which is right.

Adam: What advice would you give someone who was nervous about learning to drive?

JK: If you've got access to someone else's car, like your family's or something, just drive more and more. Drive as much as you can. Passing your test is all about ticking these boxes, but I think more important than that is confidence, so if you can get comfortable behind the wheel you can spend more time thinking about the box ticking exercises you've got to do.

And in terms of passing the test, you know, stick some boobs on your mirrors.

Adam: Of course.

JK: Speaking of funny stories involving my driving instructor, he ran me over once.

Adam: What?!

JK: When I was talking about him being an absolute lad's lad, I'd forgotten about this. So, we were driving around on a lesson and I really needed to go to the toilet, and nowhere was open, so he just told me to park up in this car park and go behind the car. So, I did, and then he took the handbrake off and rolled over my feet while I was having a wee at the back of the car.

Adam: What a lad. Lovely banter.

JK: Which resulted in me weeing all over the side of his car too, but he also ran me over.

Adam: How do you compare now as a driver to when you first started driving?

JK: A lot more competent. I used to go quite fast when I first passed. I've also been in a car accident since I passed. My friend was driving and flipped his car while I was in it. And I didn't drive for a while after that. I was only in the passenger seat but it kind of affected me. It was an old Morris Minor with no seatbelts in it, there was some problem with the suspension and I think we went across the road, hit the curb, flipped over once and then landed on its side. Thankfully we were all OK, but the idea of that happening again scared me and made me a lot more careful.

Adam: I was going to say, that's sometimes a good thing.

JK: It was, big time. The biggest thing that's changed is probably me as a passenger. I'm a lot more nervous now about being in a potential weapon, but I don't think it really occurs to me when I'm driving myself, but it does when someone else is.

Adam: Thank you, JK. Enjoy your ragu.

Lesson 3: How to Manufacture Good Luck

If I have [driven] further than others, it is by [driving] upon the

shoulders of giants.

-- Isaac Newton

Pass or fail, it's inescapable that luck will play some part in the outcome of your driving test. There's only so much you can do about that. Far more controllable are the other elements in the equation: your natural level of confidence, the variety of driving experience you get in the lead-up and the amount of time you actually spend driving.

You don't want too little time behind the wheel, but nor do you want too much either. When I was 17, my friend Simon was learning to drive at about the same time I was. He's a couple of months younger than me but he got started much quicker, with all the vigour you'd expect from a man who would go on to wear a ponytail in his twenties. His mum and dad owned a little Ford KA that would be his car once he passed his test, and that seemed to light a torch under him to get out there and learn to drive.

He took to driving well. Simon is a lot more relaxed than me. He didn't even really flap when he was 16 and held a house party at his parents' house which some bigger boys gate-crashed before going on to make a really substandard Bolognese in the kitchen and stealing one of his family's bedroom doors.

Anyway, Simon drove that KA around a lot while he was learning; to college, to the McDonalds drive-thru (the car usually had at least 10 of those cardboard cup holders in its footwells), to a now-defunct snooker hall and to Hanley town centre each Monday night for student drinking. Crucially, Simon's dad was in the passenger seat for every one of these trips, firstly to make the whole endeavour legal, but also to drive the car back to their house afterwards.

One Monday night, Simon was driving us to one of those nights out in one of Stoke-on-Trent's premier nightspots. Having already driven around quite a lot earlier that day, Simon cheerfully swung his little KA out left onto Town Road and we were chugging along for a good 10 seconds or so, enjoying the debut album of Suffolk-born hair metal specialists the Darkness, when Simon's dad pointed out, with some urgency: "Simon, you're on the wrong side of the bloody road!" Simon quickly swerved back over to the correct side of the road and tried to style it out like it was, hey, no biggie. It was fortunate his dad was there and paying attention that dad or we might have been enjoying the Darkness more permanently.

*

As you gear up for your test, it's not practical for you to drive all day, every day. Sooner or later, you'll reach a tipping point where you burn out and make mistakes, like driving on the wrong side of the road as you eagerly make your way to a foam party in Stoke-on-Trent.

Depending on your metabolism, you might also get kind of sweaty and accidentally leave a dangerously stylish pattern on your best hoodie. Not everybody can handle that.

While you're learning, your stamina for driving isn't going to be great. There's a lot going on when you're behind the wheel, and you're not used to most of it. It can sap your mental energy without you noticing. So then, how do you practice without practicing?

One way is to do what Simon did. Not the driving-on-the-wrong-side-of-the-road thing. I don't recommend that, unless you're gearing up to take your test abroad - in which case it's probably best to practice there too. But regularly going for short drives with a friend or family member can help to keep you sharp without tiring you out.

You don't even necessarily need to be behind the wheel to get some useful practice. When you're in the passenger seat while someone else is driving, just try silently reading the road as they drive around. It's not the same as actually driving, but it does help you to keep your head in the game and examine scenarios you might not have come across before. You want to get to the point where all of those micro-decisions you make while driving are second nature.

With that in mind, here are some general tips you may find useful.

*

The standard driving lesson seems to last about an hour and usually it'll begin and end in the same places - your home, your work, your college or university. The problem with that is that it can limit the amount of variety you face in your lessons.

If you have the luxury of being able to do so, mix things up when you drive outside your lessons by practicing for half an hour or so at a time - after all, that's about how long you'll actually drive for on your test. The thing to remember about this is that you don't want to only do this on the roads around your house that you're probably familiar with. If you're fortunate enough to know - or in a position to successfully blackmail - someone who'll let you drive their car (while they're in it, naturally), ask them to drive you to a place you don't know and let you drive back with them feeding you examiner-style instructions, or let you find your own way using Satnav or road signs.

It can be useful to set yourself tasks to complete by driving. Things like taking the car to the shop to pick up a dry hoodie, running an errand or two for your parents or returning a bedroom door you've borrowed from a friend. You can pick destinations at random in Google Maps if you need to, but there's just something about driving with an actual purpose that helps you to live the things you're learning. The key is to balance your time behind the wheel with any other useful driving exposure you can get.

*

Practicing with a parent is great if you have the option, but it does bring a slightly different kind of pressure. When I'd just started to take proper lessons at the age of 17, my dad took me out a couple of times on a Matalan car park and an industrial estate where I once spent a summer working in a cheese factory. We spent a couple of pleasant hours trundling around what resembled post-apocalyptic wasteland with no other cars in sight, and that was all fine. Then, the next week, my mum took me out on the roads properly, and I guess now that I had two sessions with Dad under my belt, I wanted to prove just how capable I was. It wasn't a fashion show; it would be a driving show. I was clearly a little overconfident because I remember taking a sharp bend at about 30 in 4th gear with her gripping the passenger seat for dear life. She didn't get in a car with me behind the wheel again until I passed my test.

*

Speaking as someone who returned to driving after a lengthy hiatus, I found that one good way to ease myself back into the swing of things was to sit my theory test before I'd even got back in the car. It's a much more manageable exam for starters, with its *Who Wants to Be a Millionaire?* multiple choice round followed by a hazard perception section that resembles a driving RPG.

Generally, people are much more relaxed about taking their theory test. After all, nothing can go too badly wrong while you're sitting quietly in a room, effectively playing on a road safety version of a pub quiz machine. You can also simulate the actual test quite well in preparation which helps calm the nerves. There are lots of good apps and websites out there that allow you to practice pretty much exactly the same question set you'll be served on the day. Two or three weeks of hammering the questions on one of those apps for half an hour a day should see you right.

Replicating the hazard perception element is a little trickier, but as it's geared towards replicating the kinds of situations you might see while you're behind the wheel, as long as you've been driving a little while by the time you take it, you should be fine.

One big error I made on the hazard perception part of my first theory test was that I expected my clicks to register in some way on the screen, probably because I'm too used to playing Mario Kart. Basically, just remember that when you click, nothing will visibly happen. It's important to know this as you can fail a round for clicking too many times. So, relax and try to only click once for each hazard, solidly enough to reassure yourself that it will have registered, and then just wait for the next hazard to appear.

Because I'd taken such a long break between my driving stints, I had to retake my theory test, as a successful pass expires after two years. So, I'm actually wildly successful at the theory test, with two passes from two attempts to my name. 100% conversion rate. Boom. Pleased as punch. But then of course most people only need to pass it once because it doesn't take them another decade to pass their practical test, so I guess I can't get too excited.

The good thing about getting your theory test passed early is that it effectively creates that two-year deadline for you to pass your practical test, and it also gives you some momentum. You've passed the first bit, now you just have to complete the second part. And you have 730 days to do it.

*

Another thing you can do in order to practice without practicing is watch YouTube videos. There's an extraordinary amount of dashcam footage on YouTube to immerse yourself in and pretend that it's you behind the wheel. Put one on, get in the mindset of what's going on and make your decisions and observations as it unfolds. It might sound like overkill, or maybe just a little odd, but the more you expose yourself to different scenarios, the less likely you are to get caught out when you come across an unfamiliar situation. Dashcam videos can be a real help in that. Just try not to get stuck in a loop watching only the more dramatic footage, which can normally be identified under titles such as 'BRITAIN'S CRAZIEST DRIVERS - ROAD SAFETY GONE ILLEGAL!'.

*

A slightly niche worry I used to have before each of my driving tests was that I wouldn't be able to pass the pre-test eyesight exam by reading a car number plate from twenty feet away. Thankfully, this concern is one that's easily rectified. Next time you're walking past a parked car, don't let yourself look at the plate and let yourself get 25 strides or so away from it, then turn back and see if you can read it. It's a small thing, but it's one less thing to worry about on test day.

*

Even more niche than that was the fact that I was really terrified of walking past car aerials. Every time I walked near one I was really, really worried I was going to trip over and pierce my eye and/or brain with it. I apologise if that now gets into your head as I don't have any real advice for dealing with it, but I can assure you that it's never happened to me and I'm now a lot more comfortable walking past car aerials.

*

Perhaps the most important piece of kit in my toolbox when I was trying to improve after each of my intensive driving lessons was the note-taking app on my phone. At the end of each lesson I would write down three or four things I needed to remember or do better next time, and then read and rewrite those notes ahead of the next session. In particular the rewriting helped me to internalise the things I needed to without putting pressure on myself to keep it all in my head 24/7.

Over time - and especially once you've passed your test - you learn to drive with your habits, rather than your decisions. What you need to do is make sure your habits are good ones.

Michael Phelps won one of his Olympic gold medals when his goggles leaked and he was effectively blind for the last two lengths of his swim. Because he had trained to the extent that he knew simply by instinct and habit the exact amount of strokes to get him from one end of the pool to the other, he knew the precise points at which he had to turn to avoid losing time or crashing headlong into one end of the pool. Most importantly, it meant that he was able to stay calm when something went extremely wrong on what was one of the biggest days of his professional career. It would have been very easy for him to clamber out of the pool and run away, with his coaching jogging slowly after him.

Just to be clear, I'm not looking to position myself as the Michael Phelps of driving and I'm certainly not suggesting that you experiment with keeping your eyes closed for large segments of your lessons. What I am saying is that as you encounter situations and they become more and more familiar, you'll react more fluidly to them without the need to be actively *thinking about them* so much all the time. Preparation *will* reduce your nerves. That's what it does. Practice something enough and it begins to require less and less thought.

It's a similar rationale to why Mark Zuckerberg chooses to wear the same outfit to work every day, possibly aside from a desire to be a little bit mysterious and interesting. It's one less decision to make when he has a lot of much bigger ones ahead of him that day. Every choice we make is energy we spend. This is why I suggest planning out everything the night before your test, including what you're going to wear (more on this in chapter five, but probably just go with your best hoodie).

*

TL; DR

DO get a wide variety of experience behind the wheel. It can be tempting to spend a lot of time driving only the expected test routes. This has its place, but it doesn't train your brain to react when you're presented with a driving challenge you haven't encountered. You want to learn to pass your test, but you also want to learn to drive.

DON'T feel like there's only one way of doing things. You have to find the method that works for you. If that means going against the grain, go for it.

Conversations About Driving: Kate

Like JK, Kate is a former colleague of mine, and I don't think she'll mind me telling you that she's a little bit unusual. Here are some examples:

1. Kate is a nuclear physicist, trained I believe to pretty much the same level as FBI agent Stanley Goodspeed in Nicolas Cage vehicle *The Rock*, but she has chosen to work in digital marketing with idiots like me.

2. If you work in the same office as Kate, she won't just call over to you when she wants to speak with you. Instead, she'll creep right up behind you and wait there until you turn around and then recoil in shock at her sudden, grinning presence.

3. She goes to these really brutal Rocky-style circuit training sessions that mean that for every 1 in 5 days that you see her, she'll be walking around as gingerly as John Wayne's stunt double.

She and I talk a lot about food, and often have a 5pm tea-check in the office to confirm what each other are having for dinner. In fact, when I asked her if we could have a conversation about driving for this book, the first thing Kate asked was whether it would be OK for her to eat a Thai curry at the same time. I said it would be fine.

So this conversation took place during our lunch break at work, and was notable for a moment in which Lucas, another of our colleagues, was coming the other way as Kate was walking over to my table with her curry in hand, and announced "Ooooh girl, that is a LOT of rice". Kate participated in our interview wearing the solemn expression of a woman resigned to a double HIIT session later that week.

*

Adam: OK, Kate, as I sit here and peer over this tower of rice at you, talk to me about learning to drive.

Kate: Oh, I hated it. 45 minutes before my instructor would pick me up for each lesson, I'd sit at the window sweating. I had a lot of anxiety about it.

Adam: I was quite a sweaty driver as well. Ruined my best hoodie. When were you learning to drive, then? Were you one of the people who went straight away and started driving at the stroke of midnight on their 17th birthday?

Kate: No. Because I paid for it all myself, I couldn't do it like that. It was when I got my first job after finishing university and I bought a block of five hours. I did the first two lessons as double sessions, like two-hour lessons, and then the instructor was chasing me to get the fifth hour booked in and I didn't do it because I just couldn't stand it. It was my instructor I couldn't stand, mainly. She just wouldn't tell me how to do anything. I'd told her I'd never driven a car before, but she'd have me driving along and she'd ask me to park up or take a roundabout, and hadn't shown me how to do any of those things. It was awful. Her name was Vivienne.

Adam: She sounds like a Vivienne.

Kate: What a Viv she was. I'd recommend not learning to drive with Vivienne.

Adam: Sage advice. How did you come across Vivienne?

Kate: A friend recommended her to me actually. But she didn't like her either.

Adam: Or you, by the sound of it. "Here, go with this woman who won't show you how to park up. You'll never actually be able to finish your lesson."

Kate: Oh, I've just remembered - I actually did go out driving on my 17th birthday. My dad took me to a car park and got me driving his car around, and I stalled that many times he shouted at me. And I cried. So I think that put me off for a while too. It's my dad's fault.

Adam: It doesn't sound like you had the most comfortable start to learning to drive. So, what was the trigger for getting back into it when you bought your 5 hours with Vivienne?

Kate: Well, I'd just started working, so I had a little bit of money, and I just thought it was a good time to give it a go. But then once I'd finished that course I moved back home, and then I ended up going with a friend's dad who was a driving instructor, and I went with him for almost a full year.

Adam: Hour-long lessons?

Kate: They were an hour and a half. And it was better than with Vivienne because he started me off more slowly, just practicing basic moves on car parks or industrial estates before we went out on proper roads. Effectively he got me to the point where I could move the car properly, change gears smoothly and gauge speed better before I went out for real, and that helped a lot during that first proper year.

Adam: OK, and so did you take your test that year?

Kate: Well, no. I did pass my theory test in the May of that year, and I was going travelling at the end of July, so I wanted to try and pass the practical test before I left. But then it turned out the waiting list for the practical was three months, so I was in the queue for cancellations but I didn't manage to get one before I went away, and then I had a really long break from driving altogether.

Adam: How long were you away for?

Kate: Five months, and then I came back and started lessons with a different instructor.

Adam: Was it Vivienne?

Kate: It was not. So, I didn't actually pass with my friend's dad, but he was really good because he taught you how to drive, not how to pass your test. I did like his car too. It was a VW Golf, so it had quite a lot of power, and I was insured on my mum's Fiesta, and it was such a shock going from one to the other. I'd be revving my mum's Fiesta and she'd be like, "Stop it!"

Adam: So, then you went with another instructor. How did you find that person?

Kate: She was teaching my sister, and she hated my sister, but she really liked me. Whereas my friend's dad was teaching me to drive, she was teaching me to pass my test, so she was taking me on test routes and putting me through manoeuvres.

Adam: Did it all come back to you easily enough after your break from driving?

Kate: I was fine in terms of actual driving, but it was just my nerves. I was so terrified, and I don't really know why.

Adam: I know the feeling.

Kate: But I was a student again at this point, pretty poor, so there was a bit of pressure on me to pass as quickly as possible. It took maybe two months with my new instructor and then I booked my first test, which I failed.

Adam: What do you remember about it?

Kate: Well, right before it my instructor said that she hoped I didn't get a particular examiner who worked at that test centre.

There were six you could potentially get, but sure enough I got this particular woman. And right away she had the window down and she was saying strange things like that she was allergic to my car, and other weird stuff. Honestly, she was mad.

Adam: What did you fail on?

Kate: Well, I pulled out of the test centre, and there were cars parked both sides and as I was pulling out, a car coming along the road tucked in for me. And my examiner said I'd forced them to tuck in, so that was a major. It was one of those things where it's driving etiquette rather than highway code, so it seemed quite harsh. And I only got one minor apart from that. So that was annoying.

Adam: And then what did you do after?

Kate: Well, there was quite a lot of pressure on me to pass because I'd signed up to do a work placement at a hospital in Preston and had no way of actually getting there. But basically, I had a couple more lessons, booked another test and passed that one. Second time.

Adam: Nice. What do you remember about that one?

Kate: I remember it being really horrible. It was the school holidays so there were all these kids on bikes in the road, and I had to emergency stop a couple of times because they kept coming out. It was a really, really hot day as well. I remember not knowing whether I'd passed or failed, but thinking I'd driven quite well. I think the emergency stops and general caution I had to show helped my case, because he could see that I was reactive and safe and everything. But yes, I passed with two minors.

Adam: Very impressive. And then did you get a car after that?

Kate: So, I was working by this point, and I was living miles away from the nearest station and shops, and completely relying on one of my housemates to get me around. Then just before a bank holiday weekend I went home to see my parents, and my dad asked me if I wanted to go and have a look at some cars. So, we went out, went to a couple of garages, and I saw this Ford

KA+. We went and test drove it - the first time I'd driven since passing my test - and I loved it. And then the next day he asked me if I wanted to go and get it, and he gave me £250 towards my deposit.

Adam: Trying to make amends after shouting at you for stalling in that car park.

Kate: I think so. And so yes, we went back and got my first car. I was so happy.

Adam: That's really nice. Did you give your car a name?

Kate: Daisy. I let my nan name her.

Adam: And is Daisy still with you?

Kate: My mum has Daisy now. I still see her and drive her every time I go home.

Adam: Do you still get nervous about driving?

Kate: I'm far more comfortable now. Part of it is just experience. I used to have to think about gear changes and stuff, but that's all second nature now. I can just focus totally on the road and what's going on.

Adam: If only Vivienne could see you now.

Kate: She'd be so proud.

Adam: Thanks Kate. I'll leave you to attend to that mountain of rice.

Lesson 4: How to Put Pressure to

One Side

[Passing your driving test] always seems impossible until it's done.

-- Nelson Mandela

A fun fact about me: I'm a weird sleeper. When I get into a really deep sleep, I tend to sleepwalk and sleep talk, and I have some very strange dreams. For example, you can listen to a recording of me reacting to the appearance of a little cow I'd conjured up during a particularly delirious slumber a while ago by visiting bit.ly/2V5dA9a – but probably put your headphones in first if you're on public transport.

Sadly the little cow incident wasn't a one-off. Fairly recently I had a very detailed dream in which Richard Attenborough was using his film industry contacts to cover up the terrible animal crimes that his (within the context of the dream) pure-evil brother David was committing around the world. Whenever the latest horrific nature scene was uncovered, "fixer" Richard would simply make a few calls and swoop in with the CGI footage required to frame a lion as being the one to maul that unfortunate gazelle that had looked at David the wrong way. The cherry on top being that David would later effectively narrate his own alibi over the footage on his critically acclaimed nature shows. The perfect crime. Again, I should stress that this was a dream rather than a personally-held theory.

Sleep is often an underrated ingredient in making a success of a given pursuit. The first time I took my driving test, I failed it about 10 hours before I even got in the car, simply because I just couldn't sleep before it. I was too nervous and restless to fall into a slumber deep enough to hallucinate any kind of miniature animal or celebrity crime syndicate, and so I got up in the night to read and play Grand Theft Auto on my Xbox. To be clear, I don't recommend playing a computer game based on committing car-related crimes as a driving test preparation measure in any situation.

By the time 7am rolled around I was just starting to drift into a nice sleep. But after having lain awake for the preceding 6 hours and having gained only half an hour of quality rest, it was time to get up and perform. Needless to say, I was a mess. Even on my way to the test, when I was just driving around for an hour with my instructor, I was a zombie. At one point he was making some point to me about the handbrake, and in my drained state I reached down to apply it while I was driving along at 40 miles an hour. Thankfully I caught myself before everything went Tokyo Drift, but it still wasn't the best precursor to a driving test.

It's hard to function on a small amount of sleep at the best of times, but when you have a big, adrenalising task to focus on, you're always going to be fighting a losing battle. I tried to overcompensate for my tiredness that day by drinking coffee. It's not a bad idea in theory but the problem is that the caffeine hit heightens your brain's alertness, and by ingesting more of it than normal I found it hard to recalibrate and react as I normally would, physically and mentally. Another problem with this technique for me personally is that I don't actually like coffee. I only really drink hot drinks when I'm trying to impress at a job interview, or when meeting a girlfriend's parents.

To make sure I slept well the night before my successful driving test, I decided I wanted to tire myself out with some physical exercise. I'm a keen runner so I chose to go for a 5-kilometre jog at about 7pm the evening before my sixth test.

The idea was to do enough to relax me and allow me to sleep, while not risking waking up sore in the morning. Swimming or cycling would have been even better options in terms of lower-impact exercise. If you're not sporty, go for a long walk, or if you're more of a footballer or rugby player, a knockaround with some friends the night before might work. Just make sure you don't injure yourself.

If you're not really the exercise type or don't fancy leaving the house, watching a movie can be a good way to put your mind on ice for a while before bed. A movie is good because it generally doesn't have the binge quality of episodic TV, although having said that I recently stayed up all night watching all of the Mission Impossible films and had a great time, aside from the 2 hours and 3 minutes it took to get through the second one, obviously. Don't try a movie marathon before your test though. Something around two hours in length is perfect.

Eating is also important, both in general survival terms and on the night before your driving test. Don't get too adventurous. Eat something you would normally have for dinner, and eat whatever would be a typical portion size for you. The night before your test isn't the time to start experimenting with new cuisine or innovative carb-loading techniques.

*

As you hit your driving stride, there's plenty you can do in preparation for the day of your test to give yourself an advantage, which may make it easier to relax before the big day.

For starters, there's the time of day you book your test for. When I booked my first test to take place during rush hour, my instructor immediately told me to cancel it and switch it to another day if I could. His rationale was that at rush hour everywhere is ten times busier than normal. That may not be a problem if you live in the countryside but on the outskirts of a city it can mean curveballs. One of those curveballs can be that the roads get very slow and the waits in traffic very tedious. In and of itself this isn't a problem, but your test examiner will want you to 'make progress' - and so when you're at a junction and no one will let you out or give way, it might be that the only other option available to you is to try to force your way out or cut someone up, which is of course a fail. However, if you sit there waiting for a safe gap you could potentially risk failing for undue hesitation.

It is all at the discretion of the examiners. They may accept that it's more difficult in rush hour and let you pass, but there are no obligations on them to take it into account. While perhaps unfair, it is a fact that while the conditions of the roads might change, the test marking system does not. Undoubtedly there are good drivers who have failed in rush hour conditions, and poorer drivers who have benefitted from easier driving conditions in quieter times of day and passed. Then there are those that take their test in rural areas and who are scared of driving in cities or on motorways, that get the same pass as someone who has taken their test on the outskirts of London and who are happy to drive anywhere. All you can do is book a test time to suit your strengths and give yourself the best chance of passing.

In general, you probably want to book a test slot during the day, when it's likely to be quieter and you will have a greater chance of passing.

By all means have lessons during rush hour so that you get used to the worst-case scenario with a greater traffic volume, less considerate drivers desperate to get home, and so on. That's what I did by having lessons straight after college. It will make you a better driver, but for the test get one when it's quiet. Marginal gains and all that.

*

Another way to take the pressure off yourself in the build-up is to keep your driving test a secret. There's nothing like a slew of "Relax, I know you'll smash it!" and "Don't forget to not run away in the middle of it!" texts flooding your phone on the morning of your test to heap some more pressure onto what you're about to do. If you do need to give an excuse in work or your studies, a medical appointment is always a solid reason that shouldn't attract any intrusive questioning.

Before my first three driving tests, I mentioned them to practically everyone I met. Parents, friends, classmates, people on the online forums I frequented. I think I may even have posted about it on Myspace (which was the TikTok of the early 2000s, if for some reason you're not in your thirties). I just assumed I'd pass.

Then, after getting fed up of having to tell the same people that I'd failed again, I decided to only tell my parents that I was taking my test on the fourth and fifth occasions.

On my sixth and final try, I didn't tell anyone I was about to take my driving test, not even my parents. I didn't even tell people I was having lessons again. I had the advantage of living alone at that point so I wasn't having to live a double life to propel the lie. I told work that I was doing some painting and decorating at my parents' house for a few days, and I told my parents and girlfriend that I was just using up some holiday to get some life admin done.

I'm not saying that doing the whole thing in secret was the only reason I passed my sixth test. I'm not suggesting you should do it either. But for me it did make a difference. Even parents, who want their kids to succeed more than anything else in the world, unknowingly ramp up the pressure with good luck wishes, last minute advice. I know that my mum and dad had a written-and-sealed 'Well done on passing your driving test!' card in their dresser that was bought for my first try and hung around for many years afterward. I think it disappeared around 10 years after my first failed test, at which point they must have assumed I'd given up. Having nobody know that I was trying again made it a shot to nothing; if it didn't work out, I hadn't lost anything.

I guess my reluctance with promoting the fact that I was taking my test is rooted in the same psychological issue that made my test day nerves so bad. Driving isn't that hard, but for me doing it in front of someone else was.

Feeling like I had control over the situation was key for me. It's another reason I wouldn't necessarily recommend an intense course to anyone. In another situation, I'd have probably delayed my test at the point I ran away from the car. The issue I found was that with my test date set and my days off work booked as I put in a load of practice hours in the build up to that date, it was hard to cancel all that to push things back a month. Of course, you could argue that the tight schedule ultimately forced me to act and get through it, but there was a huge amount of luck involved too. Fortunately, it was OK in the end.

If possible, try to make sure you have no other appointments on the same day of your driving test. Take the day off entirely if possible. Having to do something beforehand will undoubtedly demand some of your energy and concentration, and having to be somewhere for a particular time afterward might end up putting additional pressure on you while you're on your test should things end up running behind schedule at the test centre.

Hopefully your driving test is important to you, so try to make it the one thing you need to think about that day.

*

I guess my through-message in any of the advice I offer about preparing for your driving test is: be ruthless. Forget everything else. Be that person who's capable and for whom driving is easy. Don't split yourself into different pieces being friendly with your instructor, thinking about other things you have to do that day or mentioning things you're reminded of by driving past certain landmarks. You can have a chat before and after. But when the engine is on and you're behind the wheel, driving is all that matters.

The most important thing to do the night before your test is to make sure the next day is as straightforward as possible.

Have the clothes you're going to wear picked out and check to make sure they're clean.

Plan what you're eating for breakfast. Ensure you're not missing anything. A bowlful of dry Shreddies isn't any good for anyone.

Figure out what time you need to be awake in order to do what you need to do in order to leave the house on time. Set an alarm 10 minutes before this, and then another for the actual time.

Double check that you have all documentation that you need to present to your examiner at the test centre. Put it all in an envelope or pack it into your bag to keep it all together.

If you wear contact lenses, make sure you have your glasses out and ready as backup. Same with any medication you're taking or should be taking. You may not need any but it's best to be prepared and it's one less thing to worry about. I could feel myself coming down with a cold the week I took my successful test, so I stocked up with every remedy available and dosed myself to the eyeballs for the 48 hours before I turned up at the test centre. I felt a little dopey that morning but the medicine managed to ease most of my symptoms in time for the test. Examiners are notorious for preferring not to be coughed or sneezed on by learners.

*

Basically, my through-message to you in all of this is to be a grownup. Driving is an important, responsible thing to do, so approach it with that mindset and maturity.

When you're happy that you've done what you can to prepare and you're all set for the next day, have a relaxing bath or shower, and then go to bed - allowing enough time for you to get the sleep you need, whether that's seven, eight or nine hours.

Don't lie awake looking at your phone, even if what you're looking at is to do with driving. The best thing you can do at that point is close your eyes and get your rest ahead of the big day. Because hopefully, when you wake up, it'll be the day you pass your driving test.

*

TL; DR

DO the things that will make you feel the most comfortable. If that means talking to people about your forthcoming driving test, do it. If you think it might help you to keep it on the down-low, go for it. There's no right way to be, but do whatever will give you the best chance of performing.

DON'T take your preparations lightly. Driving is an important, responsible thing to do. The moment you don't respect it, you take a risk. Behave like it matters to you, because it should.

Conversations About Driving:

Charlie

Charlie heads up what's known as 'organic search' in the digital agency

at which I work. His team is responsible for making sure business's

websites are as naturally visible as they can be online. Once described as

"the Danny Dyer of the Cotswolds" by an astute colleague, he's very

good at his job and carries it out with the maximum swagger possible at

all times.

  While I was putting this book together, Charlie found out he was

soon to be a father and so quickly set about taking an intensive driving

course to obtain his licence. He wanted to pass his test before his wife

gave birth so that he could be the one to drive her to the hospital. I

thought I'd take advantage of the serendipity and speak with him both before and after his test. All that Charlie asked for in return was that I include a link to his website in the book, so here it is: www.whitworthseo.com. Like I said, he's very good at his job.

*

Adam: Charles.

Charlie: Adam.

Adam: How long have you been learning to drive?

Charlie: So, this time around, about a month and a half. Potted history is, I started driving lessons around four years ago, did about a year of having the odd lesson and I was in no massive rush, and then I had to stop because of a back injury. Then a couple of months ago, my wife and I found out that we were expecting a baby, so I got back in the car about six weeks ago on an intensive course.

Adam: Was it easy enough to get back into? The driving, I mean, not the car.

Charlie: It was like I'd gone back to knowing pretty much nothing. My clutch control had gone, I couldn't find the biting point, so it felt like I was starting from scratch.

Adam: And how have you found the intensive course?

Charlie: I actually like it. It really suits me, because I'm the type of person who likes to smash through things.

Adam: Probably don't say that to your examiner tomorrow as you're getting in the car. So, you'd recommend the intensive course, then?

Charlie: The momentum it gives you is excellent, and if you have a really good lesson and then you have another the next day, you feel like you're really making progress. I know there's maybe a reputation of it creating some really bad drivers...

Adam: I wouldn't say that.

Charlie: ...but for me personally it's been perfect.

Adam: How is your course broken down? For me it was three consecutive days of driving, and then my test, but there's a lot of different intensive courses out there.

Charlie: I've gone for a sort of 'soft intensive' I guess. When I found out my wife was expecting, I realised I had a few months to get it done, so I'm working to a plan made up of these bursts of three-hour lessons at the weekends and then a couple of hours pretty much every other day in the week. That's been good because it's given me a couple of days off here and there when I've been feeling overwhelmed by it. I've enjoyed the longer sessions too. There's a lot to be said for being in a car for three or four hours at a time.

Adam: I agree. The typical way of learning to drive is that you have an hour-long lesson, and your instructor might pick you up at work or at college or whatever, and then end the lesson by dropping you off at home, so there's only so far you can go in that time.

Charlie: And a big thing for me is actually getting going at the start of a lesson. Once I'm in the flow I'm fine, but back when I was learning a few years ago I'd have a one-hour lesson, not drive until the next week, and then find I'd forgotten a lot of what I'd done the last time I was in the car, so I'd sometimes be struggling with the same things. This way there's much more time to spend in the lesson itself, and then having chance to forget things or get out of practice before you're back in the car for the next one.

Adam: What's your instructor like?

Charlie: So, he's this strict Australian ex-school teacher. He's a bit of a disciplinarian, so I've not had a lot of love from him but that's probably good for me. There were no niceties on the first lesson, he was very much: "Go on, drive". But that's just his style I guess, and with it being an intensive course he's probably thinking that there's no point trying to mollycoddle me.

Adam: He sounds quite, you know, "tough love".

Charlie: Yeah, I think he's probably more critical of me than he needs to be, but I think he's doing that to push me harder and get me up to standard quicker, and that's probably the right way to do it to get me through my test in the timeframe I'm looking at, but it's been pretty tough.

Adam: Have you had any fallings-out with him?

Charlie: I mean, I would've, if it wasn't for the fact I need him to teach me to drive, so I've had to bite my tongue quite a lot. He's been borderline rude and stern at times, but I think at the end he'll probably say, "*Look, I had to be like that*". I've felt like getting out of the car a couple of times though.

Adam: I know that feeling. So, you took your theory test quite recently, right?

Charlie: This was technically the third time I've taken it. I took it twice back when I was first learning, and the first time I failed the theory part, and then the second time all of the computers crashed while I was doing the hazard perception bit, so that was cancelled rescheduled but then by the time the date came around

I'd had to put my driving on hold because of my injury, so it never happened.

Adam: But this time went well?

Charlie: I basically downloaded the app and blitzed that for a few weeks, so I found it easy this time. I'm not sure it's a great process though, the theory test. I still feel like there's loads of things I don't know, certain road markings and things.

Adam: So, you're taking your first driving test in two days, on Friday. Is there anything you're hoping doesn't come up?

Charlie: I've still not done much reversing yet, but I've got two and a half hours booked in tomorrow with my instructor to practice that and pulling up on the right hand side of the road, which I've been a bit nervous about doing so far, but it's all coming together.

Adam: What else are you doing to prepare over the next 48 hours?

Charlie: I'm going to watch a few videos of driving tests online, just so that I'm not getting into the car with the examiner on the day and not knowing what to expect, and my instructor will be going through all that with me too. The other thing for when I'm in the car is just the reading of the road, making sure I'm in the right gear and all that, so I'll be concentrating on that in my lessons. One thing that my instructor has said is that, on your test, what you're doing in the car is almost secondary to what you're observing around you and how safe you're being as a result.

Adam: I agree. I definitely made a couple of mistakes in the car on the test I passed, but overall I drove safely, and that's ultimately what counts. If you make a mistake, don't panic; just keep your head and take your time. Have you driven with anyone aside from your instructor in the car recently?

Charlie: Yeah, I took my wife out in her car last week. It's quite an old car, very different to drive compared to my instructor's, but I just wanted her to be brutally honest with me about what I was doing, how safe I was, and she helped me relax a little and feel like I'm doing OK.

Adam: That's good.

Charlie: Yeah, she's been brilliant at taking the pressure off, and if I do fail there's probably time to get another test in before she's due, so I don't need to get too fixated on passing. Plus, we have the double contingency of her sitting in the passenger seat next to me as I drive her to the hospital to give birth with the learner plates on if I don't pass! But hopefully we won't need that.

Adam: Fingers crossed. What time is your test?

Charlie: 9:12am, so I'll be doing it at rush hour in the school traffic, which might run the clock down a bit, I guess. My instructor is picking me up at 8:12.

Adam: Oddly precise times, aren't they? And it will be Friday 13th of course – are you superstitious at all?

Charlie: I'm not at all, thankfully. Hopefully though my examiner will be, and let me off a few things!

Adam: Let's hope so. You're a keen cyclist, you ride into work a lot and recently did your first 100-miler. Has your cycling experience influenced your approach to driving, do you think?

Charlie: It has, definitely – in some positive ways and some negative, I think. My instructor noticed it straight away. It turns out I'm a bit too cautious around cyclists, so whereas you might just drive straight around them, I'll end up hanging around behind them for quite a while - I guess because I know what it can be like when you're on a bike and getting overtaken too closely - so I'm working on that. But then it's benefitted me in other ways, like being really aware of cycle lanes and checking for bikes when I'm turning.

Adam: Well, safe and careful is probably exactly what you want to be on your test.

Charlie: Absolutely.

Adam: So, you're a very confident person, I would say. Do you find that your confidence is just as high behind the wheel, generally?

Charlie: So, it was quite low to start with. I've never been into cars, or driving, and I've always lived in cities so I've never needed to get my licence until now. So, I knew getting back into the car this time that I was rubbish, basically. But I've worked through that and gradually become better at driving over the last 6 weeks, so now I do feel confident and everything seems to be falling into place, but obviously I want to make sure that I don't come across as cocky on the day.

Adam: What would be your advice if I was taking my test this Friday, and feeling nervous about it?

Charlie: I'd say to practice as much as you can before it and get all of your processes down. Like I said before, the more I drive, the more comfortable I get, even if it's just going through the gears for half an hour. And in terms of nerves, it's tricky, but try to take the pressure off yourself. It's not the end of the world if it doesn't go well, and you can always take the test again. Very few people pass on their first time.

Adam: How are you planning to spend the night before it?

Charlie: Well, it's actually our work Christmas do, which isn't ideal, so I'll turn up at that for a little bit but I won't be drinking and I'll head off early, get home and probably watch some driving videos on YouTube. I'll try to get an early night, but I don't tend to sleep well when I have something big the next day, so I'll see how I go.

Adam: OK, and to wrap up I'll ask the big question. Do you think you'll pass on Friday?

Charlie: Yes. If you'd have asked me two weeks ago, I'd have definitely said no, but it's amazing the difference in mindset that a couple of good lessons can give you. Getting even the most miniscule bit of kudos from my instructor here and there now is giving me a lift too, so I'm feeling good. I feel like my fate's in my hands now, whereas maybe it didn't a little while ago. I'm not going to beat myself up if I fail, it's fine to fail, but if I had to put money on it, I'd back myself. But that's just me, isn't it?

Adam: You all over. Best of luck, mate. I'll pick up with you on Friday for another chat after you've taken your test.

[Friday morning, 48 hours later. I'm at my desk, nursing a hangover sustained at the previous night's work Christmas party. Charlie walks into the office with a face like thunder, having just taken his driving test.]

Adam: So? How did it go?

Charlie: Not very well.

Adam: Ah.

Charlie: I failed coming off a roundabout. It was the last five minutes of the test. The rest of it had been absolutely perfect as well. I'm gutted. I'm booking another test as soon as I can.

*

I have my fingers and toes crossed that Charlie will pass his next test. For now though I'm delighted to report that he's currently rising admirably to a very different type of test: parenthood. And I suspect his next driving test experience will be a breeze in comparison to that.

Lesson 5: How to Start the Day

Right

80% of [passing your driving test] is showing up.

-- Woody Allen

Great news: this is a short chapter, and with good reason. As mentioned in the previous one, the day of your driving test should be about getting you from your bed to the test centre with as little thought and effort as possible.

Treat yourself like an athlete on the day of a big match, or like Will Smith and Jeff Goldblum when they're getting ready to fly into space to kill all of the aliens in *Independence Day*. Film buffs will recall that the iconic duo don't waste a second that day completing a last minute tax return, a job application or an attempt to go viral with a particularly peng Instagram post. No, Will and Jeff were 100% focused on killing those aliens. And it's the same for you, apart from the alien bit. Your one job is to get out there and make it happen. Don't waste your energy thinking about or doing anything else.

A huge part of being successful in any given pursuit is focusing on that specific thing and committing to it 100% until you achieve it, instead of trying to do 99 other things at once and ultimately getting nowhere. For now, let anything that isn't your driving test take care of itself.

Get up at the time you figured out that you needed to, which should be at least half an hour earlier than you actually need to and have some reserve alarms set just in case. Have a shower in the time you allocated for one. Put on the clothes and shoes (/slippers) you picked out the night before. Eat the breakfast you planned to have. Don't drink too much coffee. Make sure you have all of the documents you'll need at the test centre. Put them in an envelope to keep them all together. Yes, this sounds like the kind of thing a boring, organised person would do, but you know who passes their driving test? Boring, organised people.

Also, make sure you use the bathroom as much as you can before you leave your house. This is just good advice for life in general. Remember, the wise person goes when they can; not when they have to.

I don't remember too much about the morning before I took my last driving test, principally because I'd set things up so that not much would happen. I know that I woke early, having had an early night the day before. I'd booked the day off work, so I dedicated a sizeable chunk of the morning to watching YouTube videos of people driving and re-reading my lesson notes while I ate my breakfast; cornflakes with a couple of chasers in the form of cough medicine and energy tablets. That's not a weird pre-test pharmaceutical cocktail that I'm recommending by the way. Hero that I am, I was battling a cold on the day and wanted to suppress it for a few hours with medicine and cornflakes.

After breakfasts I had a shower and got ready for Elena to pick me up. I tried to dress a bit smartly to make myself feel confident and in control. I still do this now for big meetings at work. I don't always wear my best hoody, but I do try to make an effort.

When your instructor arrives, it's a good idea to turn off your phone - or even better, just leave it at your house. You won't be needing it for the next few hours, and any rogue vibrations or alert tones from notifications in your pocket will only distract you.

Standard practice is for your instructor to collect you an hour or two before your test, so that you have some time to run through last minute practice and preparations before you head over to the test centre together. If there are any manoeuvres or specific elements of your driving that you find most tricky, this is the time to give them one more go before the main event; tell your instructor what you want to do before you set off and let them figure out a route that'll allow you enough time for each task. Then, as you tackle each one, take your time and do them as slowly and carefully as possible. There's no pressure on you at this stage, so there's no need to rush.

Because I'm a maverick and widely considered to be the bad boy of the Staffordshire driving scene, one thing I always liked to carry out before a test was an emergency stop or two. In my experience, instructors are sometimes a little reluctant for you to practice these because of the wear and tear it adds to their tyres. All I'll say is that it's your test and practicing sudden stops in the day's conditions is something I'd personally want to do if someone was going to ask me to do one in my test within the next hour.

Even if you do make a pig's ear of practicing a reverse around a corner or something, try it again straight away and ask your instructor to talk you through it step by step. Swap seats and watch them do it if you think that will help. Even if you think you've got it down, get them to coach you through it one last time. I used to feel like this was a bad thing; if I had to ask my instructor about something right before my test, how was I going to do it on my own under an examiner's gaze half an hour later? But the reality is that this is what your instructor is there for, and when you're doing the same task in your test, having their voice in your help will help you. So just stay calm, listen to them, do it right if you can and move on.

An absolutely critical thing is to arrive at the test centre in good time. Your instructor should be keeping an eye on the clock, but if you're worried about the time, speak up. Try to get there around 15-20 minutes before your test time so that you're not in a rush or, equally, not waiting around for too long.

Make sure you use the bathroom while you're in the test centre. Again, the wise person goes when they can, not when they have to. The last thing you want is to be caught short while attempting to parallel park. Drink some water as well, but it's generally best to stay off caffeine if you can - you need to stay agitation-free for the next hour.

Then, your examiner will come and collect you, and it's on. Aside from the general examiner admin tasks they'll carry out, such as checking your provisional licence and making sure you are who you say you are, they may ask (or give you the chance to request) whether you'd like to have your driving instructor in the backseat of the car for the test. Naturally your instructor will only be able to observe and can have no influence on you during the test, so generally people don't opt to do this -

but if you think it might help, or if you want to be able to hear their first-hand feedback on your test driving regardless of the outcome, go for it.

It's also worth being aware that you may have the dubious fortune to end up with not one but two test examiners in the car with you together for your test. This usually occurs when a newbie examiner is shadowing or being observed by an old hand as part of their training before they earn their full examining licence, rather than it being a case of two examiners who just really like hanging out together. It can make for an odd dynamic in the car, with you being observed doing something by someone else whose observations are being observed by someone else from the back of the car.

Thankfully it's rare for learners to end up with two examiners in the car, but it does happen, as it did to me on my second and third tests, which I of course failed. The chances of it you ending up with two examiners are very slim and the chances of it happening to you more than once are even slimmer - though made slightly more likely when you take as many driving tests as I did. Only one of the examiners is actually marking you so in theory the presence of the other doesn't affect the outcome of the test, although I suspect any margin for error that you might have at the examiner's discretion is slightly eroded when they themselves are being observed by another examiner. If it does happen, it doesn't change things too much, you still just have to drive to the best of your ability - but remember there may be slightly more weight in the car than you're used to, which could affect your stopping distance.

And then, your instructor will take you outside, and your test officially begins.

*

TL; DR

DO clear your schedule as much as you can. The day of your driving test is all about you. If you're having to split your attention and spending time thinking about anything other than your test, you're only making life harder for yourself.

DON'T hold back in that lesson before your test. Tell your instructor exactly what you want to practice and make sure it happens. You're the one behind the wheel, after all. Take control of your final preparations.

Conversations About Driving:

Sinéad

Sinéad is my Irish wife. She is in fact my only wife, but she's an excellent one so I don't mind much.

She is also the opposite to me in almost every way imaginable. I'm very logical and considered, whereas she's so impulsive and excitable that she broke two glasses, three plates and the shower within a month of us moving in together. The only thing she's yet to break is my heart, but there's time.

Even our heights are polarised, with me being 6'3 and her only just allowed to ride the Nemesis at Alton Tower. But as much as I joke, when I saw her walking down the aisle towards me at our wedding, I knew I was punching way above my weight. (Although when she got to the end and stood next to me, I realised that she was punching substantially above her height, so it's kind of evened itself out.)

Sinead and I were on holiday at the time I was starting to put this book together, so I cornered her while she was on the hotel balcony with a bottle of prosecco and a set of questions about driving. Date night goals.

Of all of the conversations about driving in this book, this one is notable for being with the person who has been driven by me more than anyone, so we touch on that a bit. It is also notable for the fact that Sinead admits to an actual crime in the course of it. If the CPS ends up needing to bring this book as evidence in the trial against her, I just hope it means that they have to buy a copy to do so.

*

Adam: Hello, Sinéad.

Sinéad: Hello, Adam.

Adam: An immediate example of the sparkling banter our relationship is built on, there. How long have you been driving, Sinéad?

Sinéad: What a great question, Adam. Thank you for asking. I have been driving for about... What age am I now? Like, 13, 14 years.

Adam: For a second there I thought you were telling me you were 14 years old.

Sinéad: I'm not.

Adam: Good.

Sinéad: I've been driving for about 14 years.

Adam: Long time. OK, so tell me about learning to drive.

Sinéad: I quite liked learning to drive. I found it quite... easy?

Adam: Arrogant.

Sinéad: Which is weird because I'm not really a technical kind of person...

Adam: I agree. I've watched you try to play a DVD on the Xbox.

Sinéad: …but I started when I was 18 and I did most of my first driving on one of the back roads at home in Ireland, either with my mum or my dad with me. We'd just go down this tiny little road near my house, get to a certain point and stop, because there were actual houses down there and they didn't want me to meet anyone coming the other way, and then my mum or dad would turn the car around and I'd drive back. And I did that for quite a while before I was allowed to do anything else.

I remember the first time my mum took me out for a drive doing that, she decided she was going to let me drive home, back to our house. There's this quite sharp little turn to get down onto the road and it's downhill, and it was my first time behind the wheel so I thought "Sharp turn, I'll have to really, really sharply turn the steering wheel". So, I did and promptly went straight into a ditch, which my mum then had to reverse out of.

So, we both learned a really valuable lesson that day. I learned that you don't need to turn the steering wheel quite as much as you maybe think you do. And my mum learned that maybe...

Adam: You weren't quite ready for corners.

Sinéad: I wasn't quite ready to graduate from straight lines, yeah. And then from there I was driving around with my mum and dad for quite a while over a whole summer, so by the time I went to do any proper driving lessons, I already knew the basics. I never had the initial driving lessons where they sort of teach you "This is how you go forward; this is how you stop..."

Adam: "This is how you avoid ditches..."

Sinéad: Yeah, so my actual lessons were straight into manoeuvres and stuff like that. I only really took professional driving lessons to learn the manoeuvres I'd need to know to pass my test.

Adam: OK, so how many professional lessons did you have?

Sinéad: About 10.

Adam: Fair enough. So, you started learning to drive when you were 18, so you weren't super keen to start driving?

Sinéad: Yeah, I had no real interest in starting to drive. The only real reason I started was because when my grandad died, my uncle got his car, and then when my uncle was going to get rid of it a few years later , and my mum suggested I buy grandad's car off him. So, before I knew it, I had this car and it made sense to learn to drive so that I could actually use it.

Adam: What was it?

Sinéad: It used to be a vibrant red. By the time I got it, it was a very faded pink 95 Corsa. It was lovely. But that's the only reason I started driving.

Adam: And of course, you were driving that Corsa around on your own for years before you passed your test anyway, fully illegally.

Sinéad: Yes, because it was Ireland in the noughties. It's different now and I definitely shouldn't have been doing it, but it was just the way. Everyone did it and no one cared.

Adam: And I now have a recording of your confession, so naturally our conversation will end with me performing a citizen's arrest on you.

Sinéad: I was under the impression I had diplomatic immunity through being interviewed by my husband for a book about driving.

Adam: I'll Google it after. Until then, that experience of driving on your own must have really helped when you actually took your test?

Sinéad: Massively. I was regularly driving around on my own, or with someone other than a parent or instructor in the car. I was driving up to university a couple of times a week, up to Galway which was 50 miles or so away, and I did that for about 6 months before I actually passed, so I was really used to driving and really comfortable doing it.

Adam: Obviously our advice here isn't for people to be driving around without a licence, but feeling comfortable is definitely a key part of the formula, isn't it?

Sinéad: Yeah, the takeaway is that you need to be driving. Get the hours in. Do whatever amount of hours they say you should do to get test-ready and then double it.

Adam: Nice. So, did you pass your test at the first time of asking?

Sinéad: I did.

Adam: That's wonderful. I hate you. What do you remember about the test?

Sinéad: I remember very little about taking the test. I remember being very nervous, but other than that I just remember flashes of just driving around. There was one bit where a guy behind me was beeping at me to go through a red light because we'd been caught behind a truck and we couldn't go through the light while it was green. And then when the traffic light changed to red the truck was going through and this guy behind me was really impatient and leaning on his horn, so I had to be all, "No, no, no, I'm doing my test, go away."

Adam: Do you think he was a plant, like they were trying to catch you in a sting?

Sinéad: It was 100% a set up.

Adam: Were you nervous?

Sinéad: No? I remember doing a lesson right before the test and that being terrible which stressed me out a bit, but then it was fine once the test started. It's like most things where you finally start doing it and if it's going well the nerves kind of melt away. You're not suddenly going to forget how to make the car go forward.

Adam: I think I got more nervous the longer my tests went on, because it was like spinning plates – I had 6 or 7 up in

the air but I was terrified one was going to drop. I felt like there was more to lose the longer it went on.

Sinéad: The examiner didn't really drag it out with me. He did have to take me into a special room to tell me the result, and I remember him going, "You passed", and then saying lots of other things that I didn't really hear because in my head I was like "Don't care, don't care, don't care, I've passed my test, give me the piece of paper!"

Adam: Did you get any good advice from anyone while you were learning to drive?

Sinéad: My mum said something quite dramatic when I first started driving. It may actually have been the day I was about to go out with her for the first time, and she suddenly went all serious and said "You always have to remember: when you're driving a car, you have a weapon."

Adam: ...as she passed you your first handgun to keep in the glove compartment.

Sinéad: I remember thinking "That's a bit over the top", but she was right; you're in control of something that can do a lot of damage. It's a bit Spiderman, but with great power comes great responsibility. And it is dramatic, but it's definitely stuck with me.

Adam: I think I've become more aware of that since I passed my test, but not while I'm driving, more while I'm a passenger. I've become a much more nervous passenger since I passed my test.

Sinéad: I think once you've started driving you absolutely do, because you're hyper-sensitive to if someone isn't braking early enough and so on. I totally judge how far people are away from the car in front before they brake, because brakes don't always work. People who spend their lives relying on their brakes are one day going to go into the back of someone.

Adam: Yeah, I think...

Sinéad: You do that, actually.

Adam: Well, you never put the scissors away, actually. So, what do you remember about *me* learning to drive?

Sinéad: Nothing, because I didn't know you the first time around, and you kept it a secret the second. I just remember you Facetimed me at work to tell me, and actually, I was already annoyed at you because there was something else you hadn't told me about at the time from earlier in the week...

Adam: My cage fighting habit? The affair?

Sinéad: Oh I remember, it was a job interview – it might have been for the job you have now actually – and two days later you rang me up and you were like "I know you're already angry at me, but I passed my driving test today", so I was sort of pleased and further annoyed. But I understand you hadn't told me because you were embarrassed.

Adam: I wouldn't say it was out of embarrassment. More of a coping strategy.

Sinéad: OK, whatever. But you did tell me eventually. It was easier for you to do it undercover then because we weren't living together. You'd struggle now that we're always in the same house.

Adam: Yeah, "I'm just going into the garage, sweetheart – back in 6 hours, and I'll probably be a sweating, emotional wreck". Can you remember the first time I actually drove you anywhere?

Sinéad: I seem to remember you picking me up from Stoke-on-Trent station, and I think it was two days before we got engaged. I was working on the Saturday, and it was Father's Day the next day, so I'd got the train to Stoke after work because we were going out with your parents the next day. I think that was the first time and I remember being impressed at how good you were, but in fairness you were doing the most straightforward route.

Adam: Still nailed it. You can only drive on the roads that are put in front of you. Did that enter your mind a couple of days later when I proposed, what a good driver I was?

Sinéad: Yeah, I was on the fence to be honest and that probably tipped the balance in your favour. What woman wouldn't be wooed by extremely cautious driving?

Adam: And now of course it's fair to say that I'm much better than you, even though I've been driving for far less time.

Sinéad: Is it fair to say that? Is that something we would say?

Adam: People are saying that.

Sinéad: You're better at parking than I am. I'll give you that. And you can also drive.

Adam: Have you noticed much difference between my driving back then and my driving now?

Sinéad: Definitely. The first time I went for a concerted amount of driving with you was when we borrowed your mum and dad's car to go to the Peak District, and you were the only one who could drive because you were the only one of us insured on it, and it was fine, we didn't crash, but you were quite nervous. There were a lot of cyclists, a lot of windy country roads and steep hills and stuff, and I don't think you were used to driving in those sorts of conditions really. It was that extra experience you hadn't had. It's made a massive difference having our own car to be honest. And you drive that more than I do.

Adam: Because I'm better.

Sinéad: Because you need the practice. I'm kidding, you're completely adequate.

Adam: You're making me blush. OK, one last question, do you think it was odd that I was really awkward about not being able to drive?

Sinéad: It's weird to me that it mattered to you so much, because it didn't matter to me that you could or couldn't drive. I think we must have been together about two years before you finally told me. You sort of framed it like "There's something I have to tell you", so I was obviously thinking we were about to break up.

Adam: It was actually a good way of doing it. In negotiation I think it's known as 'anchoring'. Make you expect something much worse to make the actual thing seem fine by comparison.

Sinéad: I guess I just didn't really know how anxious generally you were about it. You don't really have it with anything else. Had you previously told me you could drive, or had you just implied that you could?

Adam: I'd heavily implied it. I don't think I actually lied to you about it. I lied to your *dad* about it, which I feel bad about.

Sinéad: You *did* lie to my dad about it.

Adam: Which is kind of ironic, as your dad didn't pass his test, did he?

Sinéad: So, no, no, he didn't. I might not have the details of this completely accurate, but from what I understand, in the 1970s there was such a backlog of people in Ireland waiting for their driving test that the authorities just ended up giving everyone on the waiting list their driving licence. So, my dad just got a licence simply for being on the list.

Adam: I'll always have that over him.

Sinéad: To be fair, he has since passed a test, because he did one to learn how to drive lorries and trucks, so he is actually a good driver.

Adam: But possibly only allowed to drive massive vehicles.

Sinéad: Really bad in cars.

Adam: The tinier the vehicle, the more he struggles, right? Hopeless in a Mini or a go-kart.

Sinéad: Just to be clear, he's fine driving vehicles of all sizes.

Adam: Thank you very much for your time, Sinéad. I'll let you get back to your wine.

Lesson 6: How to Take Your

Driving Test (Like a Boss)

Never doubt [your driving]. Never change who you are. Don't care what

people think and just go for it.

-- Britney Spears

And like that, you're taking your driving test. It'll start with the "show-me-tell-me" question set that you'll have hopefully memorised in advance of your test. That part was one of the hardest things about my intensive driving course; because I only met Elena and got in her car for the first time three days before my test, I had to absorb a lot of that information quickly. Again, write things down, regularly test yourself and you'll be fine.

*

I don't think it's inaccurate to compare taking your driving test to running a marathon. People congratulate you for running a marathon, but - speaking as a man who once fled a driving lesson by sprinting across a Manchester industrial estate at pace - by the time you've made it to the starting line, running the marathon is the easy part.

In fact, running is a surprisingly small part of running a marathon. Nutrition, recovery, general exercise, walking, focus, willpower, positivity, planning and preparation all have a big part to play. The hard part is putting the changes in place to get you into a position where you might feasibly be able to run a marathon.

Just like on a driving test, things can go wrong. Of course they can. You might have to drop out through injury or illness, or head off too fast and ruin your plan for finishing. You might just have an off-day and not perform to your potential. But, by the time the big day rolls around, all the hard work is done - and in the case of your driving test, you're not going to become a better driver in that hour in which you take your driving test.

The reason I now know a little bit about marathons is that, ever since I realised how bad my fitness was when I tried to run away from

Elena on that driving lesson a few years back, I decided to get into running. It's strange how much running seems to reflect life.

*

I'll stop talking about running. After the "show-me-tell-me" questions, your examiner will ask you to start the engine and, when you're ready, turn out of the test centre. Before you do this, make sure you have your seatbelt fastened, give your mirrors a final check and do what you can to get comfortable. Even though it was absolutely freezing outside on the day I took my successful test, I opened the window a crack for the duration of it so that I had a constant supply of fresh air. It seemed unlikely I would fail for being a poor host with a slightly chilly car, and so it proved.

And it's an obvious thing to say, but try to relax. Don't feel intimidated by the fact a stranger is watching you drive. Your examiner is just a person. Everyone who's ever passed a driving test has done so under the gaze of a stranger. Just settle in, emphasise all of your observations and try to think of it as a normal driving lesson.

Don't concern yourself with the marks or notes your examiner is making during the course of your test. There's nothing you can do about something they've already noted down, and it may just be a minor thing they've decided to record. Stay focused. Don't split your thoughts. Just concentrate on driving as well as you possibly can.

Don't even worry if things do go slightly awry. On the test I passed, I actually stalled the car twice while trying to pull away at some traffic lights. The car was in third gear but somehow I didn't realise straight away. Nerves, I guess. That happened around three quarters of the way through the test and at that point I was pretty sure that I'd failed. Thankfully I put it out of my mind, carried on driving my best and in the end my examiner gave me the benefit of the doubt on the basis I hadn't caused a danger to anyone else. I guess that's a key ingredient to driving test success that's unfortunately out of your control; sometimes you need a bit of luck.

From there, you'll be tasked with manoeuvres, following a Satnav and handling whatever driving challenges the road and your examiner choose to throw at you that day. Like I said at the very start of this book, I'm not a driving instructor, so I'm not going to try to advise you on those things. All I can offer is some final advice on how to approach the test, which boils down to three tips:

1) Your only goal is to prove that you're a safe driver, not an experienced one. Don't take chances to try to show off just how advanced you are.

143

2) If you didn't hear or understand an instruction properly, ask your examiner to repeat it. If that means you end up passing a turning they wanted you to take, they'll recalculate their route, like a human Satnav. You won't fail for wanting to clarify their instructions.

3) Don't reflect on how your test is going during the test. If you find yourself starting to think it's going well or badly, put that thought out of your head until you're parked up back at the test centre. Don't let your mind wander from the task in hand.

*

The rest is up to you. You're already a driver. All you have to do now is prove it.

*

TL; DR

DO take your test one step at a time. You can only drive the road that's in front of you. Focus only on what you're being asked to do and what's happening around you. There'll be plenty of time to reflect on how particular parts of the test went once it's over.

DON'T panic if something doesn't quite go to plan. What matters is how we deal with those bumps in the road when they occur. If you can show your examiner that you're still a safe driver even when you're caught off-guard, you'll always give yourself half a chance.

A Letter for You, After You Pass

Your Driving Test

If you can help it, don't read this chapter until the day you pass your driving test. This is the letter my friend JK received from his parents after he got his licence, and I think it's just a beautiful thing; enough to make a grown man sob and try to disguise it as a cough. All credit for the text to JK's parents. I've changed the to/from because you're not JK and I'm not his parents.

*

Hi driver,

Congratulations!! You have now passed your driving test, an event you have waited for, for so long!

Now that you have the right to drive one of the most extraordinary objects of modern civilisation: slave, genie and magic carpet all rolled into one, and at the same time an extension of your own person, your brain, your muscles, your reflexes. You now have independence from schedules and timetables, the freedom of the open road, to come and go whenever and wherever you please.

But never forget this: you cannot escape having a fallible human being behind the wheel of your car, and now that human being will always be you. The key word "fallible" covers every frailty to which mortals are prone. It is common to emphasize the dangers of drinking and driving, but one single moment's negligence, drowsiness or wandering of attention while stone cold sober can have the same effect.

You have been taught all you should know about the control of your car, it's operation, the rules and regulations of the Highway Code, and how to handle yourself and your machine on the road. But there are other things ethical, philosophical and mechanical, for it is you who are solely the master of the machine that serves you. It is completely subject to your will. It cannot think for you or warn you. It can shout when you press the horn but it cannot see and it cannot hear; it cannot make decisions of any kind. It will carry you as directly and unfeelingly into catastrophe as it will carry you safely where you want to go.

If you ask it to do something disastrous, like overtaking on a blind bend or at the crown of a hill, it will obey. If you command it to ignore road warnings, it will carry out those commands. This marvellous, magical servant depends upon you to help it round a bend or along an icy road. If you fail it, or demand more than it is capable of, it will turn on you – and it can be dangerous.

Now too you will be called upon to protect your passengers as well as yourself, and again you must alter your thinking. The moment you have another in your car, you become akin to the pilot in the cockpit of his plane and you must accept the same obligations. Your friends and family have entrusted themselves to you and you have entered into a contract to deliver them safely to their destination.

And what about that poor, vulnerable creature that walks the highways and byways with no protective shell of steel about him, the pedestrian? You were once one of these. As the pilot of your own car will you remember your frustrations as the stream of traffic refused to wait for you at a crossing, or your terror when some speeding motorist bore down upon you?

Will you remember, now that you are at the helm of a vehicle, that walkers have a rhythm of thinking and moving different from you?

They daydream, counting their worries or their blessings as they go; lost in thought they step off the pavement without looking. Because the slightest nudge from your bumper can put them in hospital, it devolves upon you to do their safety thinking for them.

As for children, the load put upon you is even greater, and you must be prepared to accept it. There will be toddlers who break away from their families suddenly and run out into the middle of the road; older ones that chase a ball that got away; still others who ride wobbly bicycles. We will give you only one rule: when passing children anywhere within range, take your foot off the accelerator and rest it on the brake. The split second gained in stopping may save a young life.

There are thousands of motorists who chalk up a lifetime of mileage without as much as a scratched bumper. They are those who know that the moment you exceed the speed limit or ignore the danger signs, you are overruling the judgement of the engineers who built the road, traffic experts who tested it for safety and the police who may have seen people die on it.

Your best guarantee of safety is to stay alert and concentrate every moment not only on what you yourself are doing but on what everybody else is doing at the same time. You will even develop a sixth sense which will tell you what another driver is going to do before he does it, and allow you to take precautions. Experience will enable you to recognize the elements of an accident building up ahead of you, and to take the necessary steps to avoid it. It is a full time job isn't it? Why drive then? Why own a car? Because, as you will discover it provides tremendous satisfaction, pleasure and freedom.

We deeply envy you the thrill of taking off on your first trip alone, that marvellous anticipatory moment when you slide behind your own wheel, turn the key, feel the throb of your engine, ease it into gear and, your own master, move off into the unknown. This thrill will never diminish; may it bring you long years of joy and the happiness of freedom.

Your loving friends,

One Direction (including Zayn).

Lesson 7: How to Be a Great Driver

One day, in retrospect, the years of [driving struggles] will strike you as

the most beautiful.

-- Sigmund Freud

When you pass your driving test - well, that's what makes the juice worth the squeeze. Being able to take a car out on your own that first time after you've passed your test is magic. And that's when a brand-new chapter begins.

It's annoying but the cliché is sickeningly true; you learn the most about driving only *after* you've passed your test. If you think you've completed driving once you've got your licence, you'll soon change your mind. You'll still come across unfamiliar situations, you'll still make the odd mistake, you'll still come across other drivers who will make bewildering decisions that throw you a delightful curveball now and again. The difference is that you'll be the one responsible for dealing with those scenarios, because you won't have your driving instructor sitting next to you.

In my case, that's a good thing, as it means I now spend much less time pulling over and running away from my car than I would do otherwise. And the freedom and control and independence I've enjoyed as a result have made me a much more well-rounded person. I was never one of those kids who liked Top Gear or playing with toy cars, but since I passed my test I've completely fallen in love with driving.

Here's a thing to bear in mind: learning to drive is about getting to know the rules of the road, but also understanding when to bend them. Note that I'm not telling you to *break* the rules. I don't want you naming me as an accomplice and trying to take me down with you when you're up in court for driving on the wrong side of a motorway or something. Despite the hardman image I've conveyed throughout stories such as the one in which I ran away from a driving lesson, I don't think I'd thrive in prison. However, I do think a little *bending* of the rules is acceptable when it's both safe and legal.

For example, I was driving home from the gym earlier today and was hit by a green light changing to amber as I headed towards it. On a driving lesson or a driving test, that would have been me basically doing an emergency stop. Today, I just eased through while the light shifted again to red.

It's important to get to know your personal code about these things. If you're going at a certain pace and you're a certain distance from the lights as they change, you're happy to go through. What you don't want is enough room for doubt. Doubt is never a welcome passenger in anyone's car.

I'd say that it took maybe a year for me to feel completely comfortable with driving. I don't know whether that's longer than most people, but it's true. I didn't drive on the motorway straight away either. I sort of built up to that by getting used to driving on my own first and slowly building up my confidence as well as my observation skills.

I also took my Pass Plus qualification during that first year. A lot of people talk about this mainly as a tool to lower your early insurance premiums, but I learned a few important things about driving in scenarios I'd not really experienced previously. Driving in snow, in the dark and on country lanes. (Not simultaneously.)

The impact my Pass Plus certificate had on my insurance costs was negligible in the end, but the impact on how I drive was invaluable. Even if you don't fancy doing the Pass Plus, I'd still recommend some post-pass tuition to cover those situations you haven't experienced much in your lessons. Like anything, most of what you get to know you'll learn about driving you'll learn by doing, but that 10 or 25 percent of guidance can make a big difference.

I was terrified the first time I took my mum and dad's car out on my own after I'd passed my test. I probably didn't do myself any favours with the route I picked, heading right across the Peak District, trying to overtake furious cyclists on narrow, windy roads beset by some typically robust northern English weather. It gets easier, thankfully. Since then I've driven most days, for all types of journey and in all kinds of conditions. I even drove to Ireland for my wedding. Sinéad hasn't confirmed whether that was a final test before going ahead with the marriage, but neither has she confirmed that it wasn't.

Statistically speaking, I've probably been out for at least two drives during the time it's taken you to finish this book, and both probably went fine, despite the presence of other drivers. That's a big thing to still keep in mind when you've passed your test; however safe you think you are, other drivers will often be your downfall. Here are a few things that have happened to me while driving over the last couple of weeks alone:

- On my way to visit my parents a few weekends ago, I took the scenic route through some country roads, where I quickly met a man in a Range Rover overtaking a cyclist on a blind bend, approaching me at

pace on the wrong side of the road. I had to slam on my

brakes so that he could accelerate past the bike and cut

back in, or he'd have undoubtedly crashed into me, the

cyclist or some livestock in the field next to us.

- One of the only guarantees in life is that some people

  will drive around supermarket car parks as though

  they're in a dodgem or the Batmobile. I recently had to

  give someone the horn when they came hurtling

  backwards out of a space like James Bond as I was

  pootling past. Car parks are the worst.

- There were two cars parked in line with each other on

  opposite sides of the road on which I live the other day.

  It's not the widest road, but there was just about

  enough room for me to get through, so I sighed and

  went to drive through the gap. Just as I was halfway

  through, one of the driver's flicked on his engine and

  drove off, swerving into the road as he did so. As Jona

  mentioned in our conversation, most accidents happen

within a couple of miles of where one of the drivers involved lives, and it's not hard to see why.

- While I was on my way to do the big shop, an elderly man driving around a roundabout went to exit without indicating and so unexpectedly cut right across me as I went to pull out. As he sailed past, he cried of his window, "You stupid... cow" at me, a surprised bald man just trying to do his best.

- I'm not beyond mistakes either. Only the other day I reversed into a little metal stanchion that I hadn't noticed while backing into a parking bay at the cinema and scraped my bumper a little bit. The really sad part was that there were no tickets left for the two films we wanted to see, so we ended up driving home again 20 minutes later.

- I was driving home after work in the evening rush hour recently, crawling along a dual carriageway in bumper-to-bumper traffic, when I saw I was coming up to a slip road full of more cars trying to come across. I decided to try and move over into the outside lane to make a bit more room. A space opened up to my right, so I indicated and went to move into it. Instantly the guy behind the space beeped his horn and accelerated into it so that I wouldn't steal a crucial 3 metres on him. It's one of the few times I've nearly lost my temper behind the wheel, but that never helps so ultimately you just have to let these things go. If people are petty, rise above it.

- In contrast, I was coming home from a different work thing quite late at night last week and got stuck behind a guy going way under the speed limit for a long time. It was somewhat dark and foggy, and the roads were quite windy, so I just had to sit in behind him for a while. It was fine. Eventually we came to some traffic lights and he turned off, and someone behind me sparked into life and roared past me at about 80. Initially I felt a bit offended - "I hope he doesn't think it wasn't me - I was just being safe and patient" - but then I snapped out of it. For one thing, it doesn't matter what other drivers think of your driving, and for another, it's better to have those keen beans in front of you rather than behind.

Here's the thing about driving: you need to be smart enough to adapt and make decisions quickly. Let people go if they're determined to drive past you. If someone's slowing you down and you can't get past them safely, then settle in and wait for an opportunity. You'll encounter some people who drive as though they're the only person on the road. Your job is to drive like you know that you never are the only person on the road.

Anyway. We've reached the end of this particular road. You may remove your seatbelt and exit the vehicle. That's seven chapters and a few other bits and bobs on everything I've learned about learning to drive in the course of fifteen years, six tests, five failures, two instructors, a sweaty hoodie and countless hours of driving lessons. And it's all been worth it. There's so much in my life that I probably wouldn't have done in the last couple of years had I not passed my driving test, and in every area of life my confidence has snowballed ever since I became a driver. It's amazing what a cornerstone it can be.

I hope that you pass first time or next time, reader, but whatever your own journey with driving is, make sure you see it through, because it might just change your life.

Over to you.

*

TL; DR

DO what you feel comfortable with. If you're not feeling ready to go on the motorway just yet, don't. If you're not comfortable with the idea of taking a night drive along country roads, don't. Get used to driving on your own and expand your comfort zone from there.

DON'T make the mistake of believing that passing your driving test means you're a good driver, or that you're a better driver than you were the day before. Passing your driving test just means that you drove safely enough for 44 continuous minutes. Your real driving education starts now.

Epilogue

Hello again, reader. Thanks for finishing my book. I hope you enjoyed it, but most of all I hope you found it useful.

As I have made abundantly clear both on the road and within these pages, I'm not a driving expert and I never will be. However, I do believe that succeeding at something after a number of failed attempts can put you in a position to offer useful advice to people who are in the same boat you once were. And that was the purpose of this book. Even if only in the smallest way possible it's helped you or someone else to earn that beautiful pink driver's licence, it's done its job.

I'd like to say thank you to JK for allowing me to include his parents' letter to him, and to Sinéad and Jona for proofreading this nonsense to get it to the point where we agreed that it had become mildly publishable. Thanks also to Paul Gilbert for designing a lovely cover.

Finally, thank you to every person who gave up their time to talk to me about driving while I was putting this together. In the end I had far more conversations about driving than I could actually fit in the book, but maybe I'll put out an upgraded version at some point.

And that's the beauty of self-publishing a book; I can carry on sculpting and shaping it over time, rather than attempting to maintain a crate of physical copies in pen, like I assume Dan Brown has to.

With that in mind, I'd appreciate any feedback you have - how you found my book overall, whether it helped you or not and where you think it could be improved. Drop me a line at adamjmorrell@gmail.com and I'll happily listen to anything you have to say.

Safe travels.

Adam.

Appendix: My Actual Driving Test Notes

Over the next couple of pages, you'll find a full copy-and-paste of the exact notes I built up in my phone over the course of my intensive driving lessons, and which I read again and again the night before and the morning of my driving test.

I'm not including these notes as a guide to change the way you drive. They're here more as an example of the kind of detail you might find it useful to go into when writing things down to help you internalise certain things.

It's strange for me to read these notes back now. Certain things in there are so automatic to me after having now been driving for 4 years, and others I don't remember even having struggled with in the first place.

Still, it's best to leave nothing to chance, and if you're able to articulate how something should be done on paper, you're always going to have half a chance of being able to execute it in person.

BASICS

- *Mirror, signal, position. Check all mirrors before signalling to move off when parked. Always check mirror before changing speed or position when driving. Do not cause any vehicle to change its speed.*

- *Get into 3rd gear at 20mph unless speed bumps/bends.*

- *Keep at least one hand on the steering wheel at all times.*

- *Stay out of bus lanes - look for red/burgundy sections on the road.*

- *When told to pull in, check mirror and take foot off gas - look for earliest opportunity, but no bus stops and not too close to junctions.*

- *Look far ahead in the road. Take foot off the gas if a car might be about to turn right from the opposite lane - they may try and dart across.*

- *LISTEN to examiner instructions - next turn/end of road/after x/at the second set of traffic lights/at the mini roundabout. Don't make any action until instruction is over.*

- *Don't brake and change gear at same time, slow down first, then worry about gear.*
- *If stopping, don't change to first gear before handbrake is on.*

Fair self-explanatory stuff here for the most part. A reminder to keep at least one hand on the steering wheel seems like something I shouldn't have had to make a note of. In my defence though, my problem was that I had a habit of resting my hands in my lap while waiting at traffic lights, rather than trying unorthodox two-handed gear changes or anything.

PULLING IN

- *When pulling in, steer out to the right as much as you steer to the left to make sure car and wheels are straight. Don't brake too much. Use wing mirror to check distance from the curb.*

Sure, makes sense. It's strange to see this written down so granularly though, as it's something I do quite instinctively at this point. However breaking things down like this definitely helped me get my head around the logic of certain parts of driving at a stage when I hadn't practised them very much.

MOVING OFF

- *Check all mirrors and signal right.*

- *Check blind spot once, grip handbrake and check blind spot again. If clear, release handbrake and pull off.*

Again, obvious, but people do fail for not doing these things - or for not demonstrating them clearly enough. I'm not too theatrical about things in general, but I find that I still do a very exaggerated shuffle forward in my seat to peer out both ways whenever I'm edging towards a blind junction. Elena would be proud.

REVERSE PARALLEL PARK

- *Move next to car, about a door width away and indicate left before pulling up. Front of car should appear in passenger side mini window.*

- *Put car in reverse. Look around - check all mirrors and over right shoulder. Look constantly between left shoulder, left mirror and right shoulder, reversing back slowly (clutch only). Stop if vehicle or pedestrian appear.*

- *When back of car comes into middle of passenger window, one full turn left.*

- *When curb triangle meets bumper in passenger side mirror get full lock to right.*

- *When curb and bumper line up, stop and dry steer straight, then move backwards a tiny amount to make sure wheels are lined up.*

- *HALF TURNS TO CORRECT IF NEEDED - HALF TURN ONE WAY THEN BACK.*

Ignore the actual visual markers here as these are specific to me, but I definitely recommend writing down whatever yours are and which actions they relate to, as it's easy to get confused between what's needed on the different manoeuvres. The half-turns of the steering wheel thing was really good advice from Elena and not something I'd ever been told by my previous instructor, hence the capitalisation I suppose. I must have been particularly excited to document the half-turns. Naturally though, once you understand something like that, it seems incredibly obvious and you don't know how you didn't see it before. That's life.

REVERSE PARK INTO BAY

- *Position the car in middle of road between the rows of bays. Pull up next to bays with outside line of first bay running alongside chest line or 1/3 into passenger side window. Stop car and put in reverse. Look around - check all mirrors and over right shoulder.*

- *Reverse back but not too slow - clutch only. Immediate full lock left/right. Continue slowly back into space looking around. Straighten wheel when lines align with bumper. Reverse back until edge of bay lines disappear into bottom of mirror.*

- *Correct if needed - move forward and use quarter turns left/right to line up properly.*

- *Move forwards to correct if needed but don't go in empty bays. HALF TURNS TO CORRECT.*

This one is a bit harder to follow, but I'm guessing it helped to some extent. I was clearly big on this 'half turns to correct' rule though. I think I still do that. I'll check tonight when I'm parking up at the gym.

REVERSE AROUND CORNER

- *Check the road you'll be reversing into as you go past. Indicate left as pass right lane. Park straight, and don't go too far past the start of the junction - limit unnecessary reversing.*

- *Put car in reverse. Look around thoroughly and if clear start reversing back slowly (clutch only) while still looking around.*

- *At the point where the back of the car meets the start of the junction, start turning left. One full turn may be enough for wide corners, or one full lock for tight corners.*
- *Steer back right if back of car getting too close to curb in left wing mirror.*
- *Once car is three quarters of the way around the corner, start straightening wheels. If not close enough to curb, use quarter steer left to get back wheel closer, then quarter steer right to line up before straightening again.*
- *QUARTER TURNS TO CORRECT.*

Right, 'quarter turns to correct' for this one. Finer margin for error, so don't go wild with the wheel, basically. Makes sense, but worth noting down with everything else I was having to keep in my head. To be honest, I always found the actual manoeuvre part of the reverse around a corner quite straightforward. It was keeping up the vigilance to spot anyone approaching and stop the car that occasionally let me down, hence the first and second bullets.

TURN IN ROAD

- *No indication needed. Check all mirrors and blind spot before moving. Use clutch only. Immediate full lock to right, looking right and left continuously.*

- *As passenger side inside door handle gets to middle of right lane, straighten wheel and stop car. Put in reverse.*

- *Check around again for vehicles and pedestrians. Reverse and get immediate full lock to left, again looking both ways continuously. Straighten wheel as car crosses road. Stop as curb forms triangle with driver side back window.*

- *Handbrake and put in first. Look around and pull off. Continue with further instructions.*

Again, a nice simple manoeuvre but it's when your guard is down that mistakes happen, so make notes of your triggers for looking around as well as perfecting the bits where you're actually making the car move.

Appendix: My Top Five (Only Five) Driving Test Fails

Finally, as promised, a humiliating appendix of my driving test failures in full, inglorious detail.

*

Test Number 1: Went over a hump-backed bridge too quickly and, due to the presence of what I can only describe as mindless shrubbery lining the road in front of me, could not see where road was going next. So I did the most sensible thing and decided to guess which was the bend would go, got it wrong and very nearly drove through someone's fence.

Test Number 2: Forgot to cancel indicator after leaving roundabout, resulting in other drivers assuming I was taking a left turn immediately after the exit. My examiner had to slowly reach across to switch off my indicator with his finger, resulting in perhaps the most degrading feeling I've ever had.

Test Number 3: Drove too slowly when passing a line of parked cars. Was trying to show caution that someone might run out from behind one or suddenly fling a door open. It appears I overdid it.

Test Number 4: Drove too fast when passing a line of parked cars. Still not sure if I was overcompensating for my last failure here, perhaps thinking the examiner wanted to see more of a devil-may-care, bad-boy attitude to negotiating stationary vehicles.

Test Number 5: Instead of gradually edging out to check that the road was clear while emerging from a side street offering an obscured view of the main road due to parked cars, I presumably decided to spice things up by gambling that there was nothing coming, pulled out and caused another driver to have to slow down. I was about two minutes in and had only just left the test centre.

Test Number 6: Passed. Like a boss. Wrote a book about it.

Printed in Great Britain
by Amazon

34126481R00098